A GIFT FOR:

FROM:

HUMOR IN UNIFORM

★ ★ ★ ★ ★ ★ ★ ★ ★ ★ ★ ★

FUNNY TRUE STORIES ABOUT LIFE IN THE MILITARY

The Reader's Digest Association, Inc.
New York, NY/ Montreal

★ ★ ★ ★ ★ ★ ★ ★ ★ ★ ★

Copyright © 2008 The Reader's Digest Association, Inc.
This edition published in 2013 by Hallmark Gift Books,
a division of Hallmark Cards, Inc., Kansas City, MO
64141 under license from Reader's Digest.
Visit us on the Web at Hallmark.com.

All rights reserved. Unauthorized reproduction, in any
manner, is prohibited.
Reader's Digest and Humor in Uniform are registered
trademarks of The Reader's Digest Association, Inc.

ISBN: 978-1-59530-607-4
BOK1271

Printed and bound in China

★ ★ ★ ★ ★ ★ ★ ★ ★ ★ ★

CONTENTs

Introduction 9

Basic Training   11
    A Word to the Wise 14
    Meeting Expectations 18

At the Front   23
    Morale Building 26
    Pride of the Corps 30

Beating the System   33
    A Matter of Wits If Not Wisps 38

All in the Family   41
    From the Peanut Gallery 45
    Parental Pride 47
    Family Matters 48
    Service Adjustments 51
    Love 'em As They Are 55

Oops!   59
    It's Inevitable 63
    And So It Goes 67

★ ★ ★ ★ ★ ★ ★ ★ ★ ★ ★

The Home Front............................71
- Can You Cope?.................................75
- We Do Our Best 80
- It's Really Okay 83
- Homecoming 86
- Supportive Spouses?..........................90

Last Laugh................................97
- The Art of Communication 100
- Rocks and Other Difficulties 103
- Respectfully Submitted 107
- Getting Real 110

On the Job...............................115
- From the Mess 122
- In Flight 125

One Up...................................131
- The Right Stuff 135
- Military "Maneuvers" 137

Military Wisdom........................143
- Just a Little Red Tape 147
- Reading the Signals 148

Go Figure................................153
- Think Again 155
- Don't Ask 160
- Getting By 163

★ ★ ★ ★ ★ ★ ★ ★ ★ ★ ★ ★

Thinking Fast 167
So They Say 171
You Can't Win 'em All 174

Huh? 183
Another Language? 186
Come Again? 189
Some Reassurance 192

Hey, Medic! 195
Stating the Obvious 198
Use What You Know 201

Rank and File 205
Pulling Rank 209
A Rose Is a Rose 212

Credits 215

Introduction ★ ★ ★ ★ ★ ★ ★ ★ ★ ★ ★ ★ ★ ★ ★ ★ ★

Life in the military is no picnic. The U.S. services—Army, Navy, Marines, Air Force, Coast Guard, and National Guard—all require strict discipline in a rigid hierarchy. The training is diabolically tough, and that's just the beginning. The pay isn't much, and living conditions can be primitive.

Assignments can be harsh. Baghdad, for example, routinely hits 120°F on summer days. Parts of Afghanistan are snowed in for most of the winter. Missions are often not only dangerous but potentially lethal. On the other hand, when duties are not life-threatening, they can be mind-numbingly tedious.

So, how do our military men and women survive? We think a well-developed sense of humor is a key to their equanimity. It lets these put-upon heroes relieve their tensions with laughter.

All of the anecdotes in this book were sent to Reader's Digest by men and women of the U.S. military and their families. There are more than 500 separate stories of contemporary life in uniform—with its contradictions, its foibles, and its ridiculous mixups and misunderstandings. We applaud these all-too-human people who are able to laugh at themselves while still bravely defending our country.

— THE EDITORS

BASiC TRAINING ★

★ A Word to the Wise
★ Meeting Expectations

"Today, gentlemen, I have some good news and some bad news," said our platoon sergeant during our morning lineup. "First, the good news. Private Tomkins will be setting the pace on our run." The platoon began to hoot and holler, since the overweight Tomkins was the slowest guy in the group. "Now the bad news. Private Tomkins will be driving a truck."

— RICK STOVER

With his squad at attention, my father's drill sergeant began inspecting their rifles. Grabbing one soldier's M-1, he peered down the barrel only to be stared back at by a spider. "Two demerits," yelled the sergeant. "Why two?" asked the private. "One for keeping an unclean weapon," said the sergeant. "And one for keeping an unauthorized pet."

— KATHLEEN SHEEHY

"All you idiots, fall out!" shouted the sergeant at the soldiers standing in formation. As the rest of the squad dispersed, one soldier remained at attention. The sergeant stalked over and raised a single eyebrow. The private grinned.

"Sure was a lot of them, huh, sir?"

— MATTHEW HAWORTH

If he wasn't already aware of the dangers inherent in military life, things became pretty clear for my son with one look at his Marine boot camp itinerary. On one of the first days, Bayonet Techniques was scheduled for the morning. Following that: Beginning First Aid.

— TOMMY SISSON

Basic training for new Army recruits includes small arms instruction. One enlistee goes out to practice on the rifle range, where he fires 99 shots, missing the target every time. "You are the worst rifleman I've ever seen!" says his drill instructor. "What were you in civilian life?" "I repaired telephones," replies the recruit, "and I don't know why I can't hit the target. Let me see…." He gives his rifle the once-over, checks it again, and finally a third time. Then he places his hand in front of the muzzle, pulls the trigger—and blows off the tip of his finger. "Well, that answers that," says the phone guy, in obvious pain. "The bullets are leaving here fine. The trouble must be on the other end."

— SOURCE UNKNOWN

In Marine Corps basic training, I soon learned that everything we recruits used actually belonged to our drill instructor. For instance, she referred to the stuff in our footlockers as "my trash," and to the racks we slept in as "my racks." One time when we were all whispering in the bathroom while making "head calls," our drill instructor must have overheard us. To our surprise, she suddenly yelled, "Why do I hear voices in my head?!"

— KATHY VANDENBRINK

When my father was in boot camp, the troops were instructed to put their belongings in their footlockers, write their last names and first initials on the containers, and report back for inspection. A few minutes later, the commanding officer, after having seen my father's locker emblazoned with his last name "Locke" and his first initial "R," furiously bellowed, "Okay, who's the wise guy?"

— TOD LOCKE

"**W**ell," snarled the drill sergeant to the miserable recruit doing push-ups in the rain, "I suppose after you're discharged you'll just be waiting for me to die so you can spit on my grave." "Not me," replied the recruit. "Once I get out of the Marines, I'm never standing in line again."

— PETE E. MURPHY

Joining the Air Force was a dream come true. And when I sat in the copilot's seat during an introduction to the cockpit, I was eager to impress my instructor. I quickly made my way through the maze of dials and levers on the instrument panel, naming each one and describing what they did in great detail. Until, that is, I came to one with a bunch of numbers. "What's this?" I asked. "The clock," he answered.

— FAISAL MASOODI

A Word to the Wise

One of my fellow recruits at Marine boot camp looked extremely young. During inspection our drill instructor asked him, "Does your mother know you're in the Marine Corps?" "Yes, sir," replied the recruit. "Does she know you're staying overnight?"

— JAMIE WALKER

During basic training one lesson stood out from all the others: Keep your mouth shut unless given permission to talk. But I didn't realize how well our instructors had hammered this point home until one evening when we sat down to eat. My table mate started her evening prayer with, "God, request permission to pray."

— GAIL HAYES

Our first stop as new recruits was the barber's. "Want to keep your sideburns?" he asked. "Yes, that would be great," I said. "Okay, I'll get you a bag to put them in."

— JAMES MCGRUDER

Shortly after reporting to the 101st Airborne Division, we were ordered to fall out in our dress uniforms. Only problem was, I didn't know how to tie a necktie. So I asked the guy in the next bunk for help. "Sure," he said. "Lie down." Confused, I lay down on the bunk and he tied my tie. "Sorry, but this is the only way I know how," he said. "Comes from practicing on my father's clients." "What does your father do?"

"He's a mortician."

— HOWARD MARSHALL

One day in artillery instruction, a colonel came to inspect our class. First up was Private O'Malley. The colonel got in his face and asked him what reading he had on his 105 mm howitzer. "Two-nine-oh-seven, sir," was the reply.

"Soldier," said the colonel, "don't you know you never say "oh" in the artillery? You say "zero." What's your name, soldier?" "Zero Malley, sir," answered the private.

— JOHN MADSON

Short and baby-faced, my buddy Wiggins had trouble being taken seriously in the Army. A mustache, he assumed, would fix that. He was wrong. "Wiggins!" bellowed our drill instructor after spotting the growth during inspection.

"What's so special about your nose that it's got to be underlined?"

— K. TROTT

Basic training has a way of making a soldier feel that he or she is being worked like a dog. Now I have proof. While on KP duty at Fort Leonard Wood in Missouri, I was hauling containers of vegetables. On the side of one box was this: "FOR ANIMAL OR MILITARY USE ONLY."

— LORI MONTGOMERY

During a field exercise at Camp Lejeune, N.C., my squad was on a night patrol through some thick brush. Halfway through the exercise, we realized we had lost our map. The patrol navigator informed us, "Our odds are 1 in 359 that we'll get out of here." "How do you come up with that?" someone asked. "Well," he replied, "one of the degrees on the compass has to be right."

— K. S. MCGUIRE

While being transported to basic training as a new enlistee of the Air National Guard, I accidentally opened a parachute in the rear of the C-47. The plane was piloted by a major and a captain, and I felt intimidated as I opened the cockpit door to confess what I had done. Expecting to be severely chastised, I was surprised by the captain's calm response. "Well, son," he said, "if this plane goes down, that chute is yours."

— JAMES KUHNZ

My grandson, Will, called home from West Point one evening and complained about how difficult the training was. When his father told him to try to find something positive, Will mentioned how he liked to spit-shine his boots. "Really?" his father said. "Why?" "Because," Will replied, "that means my feet aren't in them."

— PAULINE CANDA

During basic training, my platoon was given a choice of going either to the gym or the PX. By a show of hands, we opted for the PX. "Uh-uh," said our sergeant. "You're all going to the gym." "But, Sarge," whined one recruit, "we took a vote." "Boys, let me explain," he said. "We're here to defend democracy, not practice it."

— WARREN PANSIRE

> After enlisting in the Navy, a friend of mine found himself in basic training learning about firearms. He was aided by a sticker on his rifle with an arrow pointed toward the barrel. It read: "Point This End At Enemy."
>
> — BRIANNA SCANLON

"Miserable" doesn't begin to describe how my troops and I felt during two weeks of maneuvers. Aside from grueling training, we camped outside under austere conditions, in often severe weather. So on our last Sunday morning, I was heartened to see many of the enlisted men standing single file waiting to enter a small local church. "A little of that old-time religion?" I remarked to the first sergeant. "No, sir," he said. "Flush toilets."

— MICHAEL CAMPO

Meeting Expectations

After enlisting in the 82nd Airborne Division, I eagerly asked my recruiter what I could expect from jump school. "Well," he replied, "it's three weeks long." "What else?" I inquired. "The first week they separate the men from the boys," he said. "The second week they separate the men from the fools." "And the third week?" I asked. "The third week the fools jump."

— TOD REJHOLEC

You've never seen two greener recruits than Fred and me the day we arrived for basic training. We were immediately assigned guard duty, and soon after, Fred was approached by an officer. "Halt! Who goes there?" Fred shouted. The officer identified himself and waited for a response. And waited … "What's wrong, soldier, don't you remember what comes next?" "No," Fred yelled back. "And you're not taking another step until I do."

— L. EDMOND WOLFE

★ ★ ★ ★ ★ ★ ★ ★ ★ ★ ★

While in Marine Corps boot camp, we were taught to keep our heads if taken prisoner by the enemy. After all, methods used to extract information, we learned, might not be the ones we were expecting. "Imagine that the door to your cell opens and in walks a beautiful young woman in a revealing outfit," said our instructor. "The best thing to do is not to touch her." From the back of the room came the question, "Sir, what's the second best thing?"

— DAVID GRAVES

Being a career soldier was not in the cards for one particular recruit. Every time he took his turn at the rifle range, he'd lift his rifle, aim at the target, fire— and hit some tree way off in the distance. One day, despondent after claiming a number of trees but no targets, he said to the sergeant, "I think I'll just go and shoot myself." "Better take a couple of extra rounds," the sergeant shot back.

— MANUEL G. RODRIGUEZ

My brother and I arrived at boot camp together. On the first morning, our unit was dragged out of bed by our drill sergeant and made to assemble outside. "My name's Sergeant Jackson," he snarled. "Is there anyone here who thinks he can whip me?" My six-foot-three, 280-pound brother raised his hand and said, "Yes, sir, I do." Our sergeant grabbed him by the arm and led him out in front of the group. "Men," he said, "this is my new assistant. Now, is there anyone here who thinks he can whip both of us?"

— ROBERT NORRIS

 No, Ferguson, the military does not have **Casual Fridays!**

During flight school, our instructor noticed that a young pilot wasn't wearing her earplugs correctly. "If you don't fix your earplugs, you'll turn into a deaf old man like me," he warned over the roar of helicopter engines. She shot back, "If I turn into a deaf old man, I've got bigger problems than hearing loss."

— DEBORAH GATRELL

For some recruits, there is nothing basic about basic training. It was clear that one soldier in particular was not getting the hang of it when on guard duty one night, he cried out, "Halt! Don't shoot or I'll move!"

— TOM BIRDWELL

A recruit in Navy boot camp got on the wrong side of our company commander and was ordered to do push-ups. As he neared triple digits, an airliner flew overhead. "I bet you wish you were on that plane, don'tcha?" sneered the CC. "No, sir," said the unlucky recruit. "Why wouldn't you want to be on that plane?" "Because," the recruit grunted between push-ups, "that plane's landing. I want to be on one that's leaving."

— GENE DAMRON

After about three weeks in basic training, my husband's unit was not measuring up to expectations, and the sergeant threatened to send them all back three weeks to start over. Apparently, at least one new soldier was already reconsidering his career choice. As the sergeant's threat hung in the air, an anonymous voice called out, "How about sending us back four weeks?"

— DEBORAH FRANK

Shortly after joining the Army, I was in line with some other inductees when the sergeant stepped forward with that day's assignments. After handing over various tasks, he asked, "Does anyone here have experience with radio communications?" A longtime ham operator, I shouted, "I do!" "Good," he said. "You can dig the hole for the new telephone pole."

— DON KETCHUM

One month into Marine Corps training in San Diego, Calif., we were preparing for a ten-mile march in 100-degree weather when a jeep drove up with a large radio in the back. "Who knows anything about radios?" our drill instructor asked. Several hands went up, and anticipating a ride in the jeep, recruits began listing their credentials. Everything from a degree in communications to a part-time job in a repair shop was declared. The DI listened to all the contenders, then pointed to the most qualified. "You," he barked. "Carry the radio."

— JIM SAPAUGH

After a grueling day of training, which had included a ten-mile hike and completion of a difficult obstacle course, my son Eric's platoon of raw recruits quickly fell into bed. As Eric lay in the dark, he heard a voice recite a prayer: "Now I lay me down to sleep, I pray the Lord my soul to keep, if I should die before I wake, thank you, Lord." There was a brief pause and then several voices said in unison, "Amen."

— ROBERT MOORE

AT the FRONT

★ Morale Building
★ Pride of the Corps

As if being sent off to war-torn Somalia in the '90s weren't nerve-racking enough, there were also the bugs. "Sergeant," I called out during our orientation briefing, "is there a problem with scorpions here?" "No need to worry about scorpions, Captain," he assured me. "There are enough snakes around to eat most of them."

— CAPT. M. A. NIXON

In the final days before our massive ground attack on Iraq in Operation Desert Storm, my tank company was moved to a position 15 to 20 kilometers from the Iraqi border. It was a very flat, open area that left us vulnerable to Scud missile attacks. Therefore, every evening we repositioned one kilometer to make targeting more difficult. It meant tearing down tents, camouflage nets, communications gear, barbed wire and more, only to reassemble it ten minutes later in a new location. Since we had other units to our south, east, and west, the only direction we could move was north, closer to the border. As a young company commander, I knew that my soldiers hated this routine. One day I asked a small group of soldiers if they understood why we relocated every night. "Yes, sir," came the confident reply of one soldier. "We're sneaking up on them!"

— DAVID C. STADER

As we drove our refueling truck through a heavily bombed-out area of Iraq, I spotted an unexploded shell in the middle of the road. "Look out!" I yelled to my friend who was driving. But he wasn't the least bit concerned. "Don't worry," he said. "It's one of ours."

— SHAD ALEXANDER

During the Persian Gulf War, my Marine Corps unit had to dig new foxholes every time we changed positions. Once, when a private was making his trench, he complained to our sergeant, "Why do we have to do this stupid digging?" Then there was a loud explosion a hundred feet away. "What was that?" asked the private. "That," replied the sergeant, "is called incentive."

— MICHAEL MERRELL

Our daily routine aboard the USS *Trenton* off the Somali coast, transporting Marines and their cargo to and from shore, was disrupted by a visit from an admiral. I was in charge of the ensign, a huge, 30-by-50-foot American flag. After the admiral gave his speech and left, the ensign was to be lowered. I had folded our national flag many times, but never one of this immense size. Fortunately, a group of Marines nearby was quick to help. One of them, Ramirez, immediately took charge, showing great pride with every meticulous fold. "Where did you master the art of folding a flag this size?" I asked. "Are you on a special flag detail?" "Actually," said Ramirez, "I learned this while working at McDonald's."

— SAM RICKABAUGH

Western Iraq is a dangerous place, so the arrival of my flak jacket was a welcome sight. What was less welcome was the sight of these words someone had written on the ceramic plates that made up the inside of the jacket:

"Fragile! Handle with Care."

— NIC EVANSO

AT THE FRONT ★ 25

A few years ago I worked as a radio operator with the Second Infantry Division in Korea. Traffic over the radio came fast and furious, and it became apparent early on that handling it all was a special skill. During one particularly hectic day I took a break and walked past another unit, where an operator calmly manned three radios while flawlessly taking down messages. Later I ran into the soldier and remarked how impressed I was with his cool efficiency. "What's your secret?" I asked. "I had training as a civilian," he responded. "I worked the McDonald's drive-through."

— GREGORY LIPE

Morale Building

Serving in Afghanistan is, as might be expected, very stressful. So another soldier and I built a horseshoe pit to help ease the tension. When our sergeant came by to play, everything was in place except for one thing. "Aren't you going to put in the stakes?" he asked. "Nope," I answered. "Fine, I'll do it myself." "Okay," I said. "But remember, this is one of the most heavily land-mined countries in the world." "You're right!" he said, gingerly stepping out of the pit. "I'll get the new lieutenant."

— JASON GARDNER

Our division had to repaint our Humvees to a sand color for Desert Storm. The result was a pinkish hue, and the jokes began. One wag renamed us the Pink Panzer Division. But the best was the Humvee bumper sticker "Ask me about Mary Kay."

— DAVID K. DRURY

 Okay, we'll meet back here at 1600 hours. Synchronize your **BlackBerries.**

My cousin was attached to a Marine air squadron that was deployed with an Air Force fighter unit flying missions over Bosnia. When the Marines arrived at the air base in Italy, they were ordered to move into a camp in a field near the runway. The Air Force unit soon followed, but their pilots checked into a hotel. Shortly afterward an Air Force colonel drove to the Marine camp. "Hey, Marines," he called out, "start breaking camp." "Are we moving into the hotel with you?" the Marines asked. "No," the Air Force colonel joked. "We need you to move your tents off of what's going to be our golf course."

— W. C. GRAHAM

At the end of a tough day in Iraq, my daughter the airman collapsed onto the first seat in the transport truck, forcing everyone else to climb over her. "Private!" hollered the sergeant. "Skinny girls get in the back so when we men get on with our weapons and equipment, we don't have to climb over you. Have I made myself clear?" Suddenly my daughter perked up, responding, "Do you really think I'm skinny?"

— MARGARET CULBERTSON

The boyfriend of a co-worker is serving in Iraq. Naturally, she can't wait for him to come home. "How's it going over there?" I asked her. "He e-mailed me last night," she said. "It's quiet where he is." Knowing that doesn't make it any less scary, I asked, "What outfit is he serving in?" "Desert camouflage."

— GEORGE COVELES

To mail a big package of cookies to my two Air Force sons, both of whom were serving in Saudi Arabia, I was required to attach a label describing the contents. I carefully marked the box "Cookies" and sent it off, but after a month my sons said they had yet to receive my package. Suspicious, I baked another batch, only this time I labeled the contents "Health Food." Within a week my sons reported they had received the goodies.

— WANDA HAMEISTER

While serving in Korea, I took a course in rappelling. As the only noninfantryman in the group, I felt pressure to perform as well as the "ground pounders." In our first class we were told to hook up to a rope and jump off a 50-foot tower. As each student nervously went over the edge, we were encouraged to shout morale-building slogans. Ahead of me I heard cries of "Geronimo," "Airborne" and "Air Assault." Being a postal clerk, I got a round of laughs when I jumped from the tower and shouted, "Airmail!"

— PHILIP PETERS

Before shipping out to Europe with the Army Air Corps during World War II, my father loaned his buddy $20. The two were assigned to different units and lost contact. Months later, my father's plane was shot down. Bleeding from shrapnel wounds, he bailed out and was greeted by German soldiers, who took him as a prisoner. After a long train ride, little food and days of forced marching, he arrived at his assigned stalag. As he entered the compound, he heard a familiar voice. "You cheapskate! You followed me all the way here for a measly $20?"

— BRUCE EY

Since I'm at a base in Korea, my family has to stay behind in the States. Every package I get from them comes with a customs form listing the contents and their value. Once, I got a box from home. The contents listed on the form read: "Homemade chocolate chip cookies." In the space marked "Value," my wife wrote: "Priceless."

— JON SUTTERFIELD

Using sand from quarries in Kuwait, Navy Seabees stationed in Al Jaber Air Base were building concrete aircraft parking ramps before the start of Operation Iraqi Freedom. When the quarries were closed temporarily, our stockpiles were exhausted in three days. The fourth day the following report was issued: "Kuwait has run out of sand."

— JOHN LAMB

Pride of the Corps

I was participating in a U.N. peacekeeping mission outside Skopje, Macedonia. We were required to stay on post at all times, so I hadn't been off base for six weeks when a general came to boost morale. Speculation ran high over who would be invited to the general's dinner at a top restaurant in Skopje. The afternoon of the big event, my commander called me over and said, "Captain Adams, you know the dinner we're having for the general?" "Yes, sir!" I replied, expectantly. "Well, the general forgot to bring civilian clothes," he said. "You're about his size. Can he borrow a pair of pants?"

— THOMAS R. ADAMS, JR.

As he prepared to leave for the Gulf, my husband was complaining to a friend about his uniform. Military men are taught to care about their appearance, and the Air National Guard would be wearing desert camouflage but not the matching sand-colored utility belt. "I get it," said his friend. "You always want to look your best, even when you don't want to be seen."

— LISA RAINO

When the Second Division set up shop in South Korea, it did so with its slogan proudly displayed at the front gate: "Second to None." A few months later, a South Korean base opened two miles down the road. The sign greeting visitors read "You are now entering the famed sector of the South Korean ROK Division, better known as 'The None Division.' "

— LUCION CLEMONS

We were asleep in our cots at Bagram Air Base in Afghanistan when exploding enemy rockets woke us up. My platoon and I threw on our fatigues, grabbed our weapons and ran to the bunker for protection. Inside the bunker, one nervous soldier lit up. "Put that cigarette out!" I ordered. "Yeah, forget the rockets," said another soldier as more rounds rocked the bunker. "That secondhand smoke'll kill ya."

— SSG JAMES KELLERT

At an Air Force symposium, a colonel gave a briefing on military activity in the Persian Gulf. "The first slide shows the area in which we were operating," the colonel began. Then he realized the slide was in backward. There was a pause as the projectionist flipped the map around. "As you can see," the colonel continued dryly, "our first and constant concern was the region's instability."

— ANDY SMITH

In Korea, a number of fellow Marines who were raised in the country told those of us from the city how delicious roasted pheasant was. They even persuaded our cook to make the dish, should we be lucky enough to find a few birds. Driving in the countryside soon afterward, I spotted one of them in a tree about 200 yards away. I immediately shot the bird, jumped over a fence and ran across the field to retrieve it. When I got back to my jeep, there were two military policemen waiting for me. I explained what I had done and why, but the sergeant still scowled. "You made two mistakes, son," he said. "First, that's a hawk, not a pheasant. Second, you just ran through a minefield."

— LAWRENCE L. VOYER

BEATING the SYSTeM

 A Matter of Wits If Not Wisps

Impressed by how well Airman Jones gets recruits to sign up for GI insurance, the captain listens in on his sales pitch. "If you have insurance and are killed in battle, the government pays $50,000 to your beneficiaries," explains Jones. "If you don't have insurance and get killed, the government pays nothing. Now," he concludes, "who do you think gets sent into battle first?"

— SGT. KENNETH J. ALMODOVAR

A few years ago, with the Fourth of July approaching, it was my job as safety officer of my Marine Corps unit to develop a slogan and to put up posters discouraging drinking over the holiday weekend. We had no accidents that year, and I attribute it partly to our slogan: "He who comes forth with a fifth on the Fourth may not come forth on the fifth."

— ROBERT ABNEY

I was stationed at Sheppard Air Force Base in Texas when I was told I would have to qualify to use a .38-caliber pistol. Having only held a gun on two other occasions, I was apprehensive. When I fired my first shot, the loud bang and the gun's kick startled me so much I almost dropped the pistol. Worst of all, in my panic I forgot to keep the gun pointed down range and drew a stern reprimand from my sergeant. When I retrieved my targets, however, I was amazed to see that I had qualified with flying colors. The sergeant looked at my scores with disbelief and commented that he had been certain I would fail. Smiling, I held up my index finger and thumb in a mock gun position and said, "Nintendo."

— PEGGY ALSTON

Some pet peeves with soldiers: Finding out the "C" in C rations stands for "cat." You're on amphibious maneuvers and you just can't stop giggling. Marching with fixed bayonets and the guy behind you doesn't hear "halt!" Mediocre in-flight magazine on troop transports. Whenever you screw up, somebody starts singing that "Be All That You Can Be" song real sarcastically.

— SOURCE UNKNOWN

A friend whose husband was stationed at Fort Bliss, in Texas, actually got a letter addressed to "Fort Ignorance." "How did you know where to deliver it?" she asked the mailman. "We were stumped at first," he admitted. "But then I remembered, "Ignorance is bliss."

— WILLIAM DE GRAF

The guard in Air Force basic training must check the ID of everyone who comes to the door. A trainee was standing guard when he heard a pounding on the door and the order "Let me in!" Through the window he saw the uniform of a lieutenant colonel and immediately opened up. He quickly realized his mistake. "Airman! Why didn't you check for my authority to enter?" Thinking fast, the airman replied, "Sir, you'd have gotten in anyway." "What do you mean?" "Uh … the hinges on the door … they're broken, sir." "What? Show me!" With a twinkle in his eye, the airman opened the door, let the officer step out and slammed the door shut. "Airman! Open up immediately!" "Sir, may I see your authority to enter?" The airman was rewarded for outsmarting his commanding officer.

— ROSS BALFOUR

In the early '90s, when I was stationed at Caserma Carlo Ederle in Italy, it was very common to see soldiers riding bicycles back and forth to work. So it came as no big surprise that, after a series of painfully comic accidents, a new policy was announced, saying in summary, "Soldiers shall no longer salute officers who are engaged in the riding of a bicycle."

— MICHAEL TEAS

My boss is a public-affairs manager who is called at all hours of the day to solve various problems for clients. But as a Naval Reservist, he was summoned to the Persian Gulf War for an extended time, leaving me to explain that he was serving his country halfway around the world and therefore could not be reached. Most callers understood, but one was indignant. "Can he be paged?" the man inquired. "I don't think you understand," I said in my most patient voice. "He's serving on a ship in a war zone." "I see," the man said. "Do you think he will be calling in for messages?"

— SUSAN HULL

Fifteen years of blissful civilian life ended when I re-upped with the Air National Guard recently. It took time getting back into the swing of things, and after a particularly rough day I missed chow, which meant dinner would be a dreaded MRE: Meal Ready to Eat. As I sat on my bunk staring at "dinner," I said to a far younger airman, "Well, I guess we just have to get used to roughing it." "Dude, tell me about it," he said. "We only get basic cable!"

— KINGSLEY SLONE

★ ★ ★ ★ ★ ★ ★ ★ ★ ★ ★

My husband and I were stationed at Marine Corps Air Station, Cherry Point, N.C., where he worked with top-secret communications equipment. One afternoon I watched as he and three other Marines struggled to set up a huge screen that looked like a television. After they finished, I asked my husband if he was permitted to tell me what the screen was for. He said that it would be used for communications, but that the higher ranks couldn't know its intended use. Confused, I asked, "Is it that top secret?" "No," he replied, "we're gonna use it to watch football games."

— J. L. SABIN

★ ★ ★ ★ ★ ★ ★ ★ ★ ★ ★

Soon after graduating from the Primary Leadership Development Course at Fort Campbell in Kentucky, I bragged to my first sergeant about how well I did in the land-navigation exercise. Looking at me skeptically, the first sergeant handed me a map of the base, a compass and a set of coordinates. Then he ordered me to find his designated point and call in. When I reached the coordinates, it turned out to be the PX. I found a pay phone and contacted the first sergeant. "Great job!" he declared. "Now that you're there, could you bring me some lunch?"

— ROBERT WIDO

A Matter of Wits If Not Wisps

How do you stop a thief? This was the question that vexed my brother-in-law, a rugged Marine. Every morning he picked up coffee from Starbucks, and every morning that cup of coffee mysteriously disappeared from his desk. Although he never caught the bandit, he did resolve the matter. One morning, when all personnel were gathered for a staff meeting, he popped out the partial plate from his mouth and swished it around in his coffee before placing it back. His coffee was never stolen again.

— JEAN SHORT

A senior in the high school class I taught was always in trouble, both at home and at school, and he was getting fed up. "That's it! I'm tired of people telling me what to do," he announced one day. "As soon as I graduate, I'm joining the Marines."

— DENNIS BRESNAHAN

★ ★ ★ ★ ★ ★ ★ ★ ★ ★ ★

While delivering a motivational lecture to a group of young Navy men, I spoke in great detail about why I joined the military and how much it meant to me. Finishing my story, I pointed to a young, sharp-looking sailor and asked him why he decided to go to sea. "Well, Chief," he said, "When my old man put lights on the tractor, I knew it was time to leave the farm."

— BILL CROCKETT

My husband, a U.S. Coast Guard pilot, was on an exchange tour with the Royal Navy in England. Everyone who drove through the base's gates was required to hold an official ID card up to the windshield for inspection by the guards. As a friendly competition, my husband's squadron started flashing different forms of ID, such as a driver's license, just to see how far they could go to fool the busy guards. The winner? The fellow who breezed past waving a piece of toast.

— ELIZABETH M. LANGE

I served with a guy who did a strange thing: He bounced an imaginary basketball wherever he went. Eventually, a psychiatrist labeled him unfit for duty, which led to a medical discharge. After the proceedings, he addressed the officer in charge. "Sir, may I approach?" With permission granted, he went through the motion of putting something on the officer's desk. "What is this?" asked the officer. "My basketball. I don't need it anymore."

— SOURCE UNKNOWN

BEATING THE SYSTEM ★ 39

When a ship enters a port, special permission must be given for sailors to begin their liberty early. My friend had a good reason for getting a head start. "I have to go to the bus station," he told a superior officer. "I have a one-armed uncle coming to town with two suitcases." Permission was granted.

— N. U. TURPEN

One of the fighter pilots at my base in England, tired of being kidded about his baldness, tried one worthless miracle cure after another. Finally he settled for growing his remaining hair long and combing it over the top of his head. The taunts continued, however, until the day they were overheard by a visiting general. Walking up to the pilot, the general soberly commended him for adopting the official Air Force solution to his problem. Then, turning to the tormentors, the general removed his hat to reveal three wispy strands of hair carefully combed over an otherwise bald pate. "This, gentlemen," he said with a smile, "is what we call tactical redeployment of available forces."

— FRANCESCA BARTHOLOMEW

I was talking on the phone with my son, who was stationed in Hawaii with the Air Force. He was explaining how the troops were learning to scuba dive. They used the buddy system, he said, and occasionally dived into shark-infested waters. Listening on the extension, my daughter asked, "What do you do when you see a shark?" Said my son, "Swim faster than my buddy."

— JOAN NOZKOWSKI

ALL in the FAMILY

★ **From the Peanut Gallery**
★ **Parental Pride**
★ **Family Matters**
★ **Service Adjustments**
★ **Love 'em As They Are**

★ ★ ★ ★ ★ ★ ★ ★ ★ ★ ★

My husband was a Navy chaplain deployed to the Persian Gulf at the end of Desert Storm. I did everything possible to ensure that our three young children wouldn't be worried about their father being in danger. It wasn't always easy, but I knew I'd succeeded when someone at church asked our three-year-old where his dad was. My son replied, "He's in Persia, golfing."

— MARSHA HANSEN

When I tell people that I am an explosive ordinance disposal technician, I usually need to go into further detail about what I do. Once I was with my eight-year-old son when I was explaining my job to someone. "I defuse live bombs," I said. "Yeah," my son added. "If you see him running, you'd better catch up!"

— THOMAS LIGON

I knew I had been in the military too long when my five-year-old daughter sang her version of "Silent Night." It went like this: "Silent night, holy night, all is calm, all is bright, Round yon virgin mother and child, Holy infantry, tender and mild…."

— MIKE ADAMS

Since I grew up in the civilian world, I knew my daughter's childhood as a military brat would be drastically different from my own. This became quite apparent one day when a playmate arrived and asked my daughter, "Wanna play commissary?"

— LORI A. BURDETTE

One day while stationed at Fort Stewart, Ga., I drove onto the base with my five-year-old son, Michael. It was approaching 5:00 P.M., and traffic came to a halt because it was time for taps. We stopped right in front of the field where the flag ceremony was taking place. The bugler played, the cannon boomed and the flag came down. "Mom," Michael said with surprise, "the only way they can get the flag down is to shoot it?"

— CRYSTAL D. FRANQUEZ

As a woman in the Marines, I often don't feel as feminine as when I had a civilian job in which I wore dresses and left my hair down. One day I was feeling especially depressed about this and couldn't wait to get home to change. When I arrived, I found that my friend and her 18-month-old daughter had been waiting for me. My friend is married to a Marine, and my worries about appearing less than feminine only increased when her little girl glanced up at me and yelled happily, "Daddy's home!"

— TIFFANY EVANS

Just before I was deployed to Iraq, I sat my eight-year-old son down and broke the news to him. **"I'm going to be away for a long time,"** I told him. **"I'm going to Iraq." "Why?"** he asked. **"Don't you know there's a war going on over there?"**

— THOMAS CIOPPA

 Not bad kid, but you'd be vulnerable **to attacks** here and here.

Teaching second graders at our base school, I showed photos of Greek ruins, including the Acropolis, Mycenae and Corinth. "Any questions?" I asked afterward. One boy raised his hand. "Who bombed them?"

— KATHLEEN CORMACK

One day a fellow Coast Guard Auxiliary member delivered a water-safety speech to a group of Brownies. Having served a career in the Air Force before joining the auxiliary, he wore a chestful of award ribbons. After his talk a little girl in the front row raised her hand and asked him how he had gotten so many medals. My friend pointed to the top half and said, "The Air Force gave me these." Then he pointed to the lower half and said, "The Coast Guard gave me these." The little girl paused, frowned and replied, "In the Brownies, we have to earn them."

— SOURCE UNKNOWN

From the Peanut Gallery

My son-in-law, Carlos, stationed at March AFB in California, was deployed to Saudi Arabia for three months. Before leaving his wife and three young children, he sat down with four-year-old Andrew. "I'm going to be gone a long time," he said. "While I'm away, you're going to have to be the man in the family. You'll have to take care of your younger brother and sister. There are lots of things you can do around the house." The more he talked, the bigger Andrew's eyes got. Finally Andrew turned to his mother and said, "You'll have to help."

— JOSEPH P. MCPARLAN

★ ★ ★ ★ ★ ★ ★ ★ ★ ★

We had just moved to an Army post from an Air Force base and my young son, an avid fan of GI Joe toys, was excited to see the troops marching in cadence. An even bigger thrill came when he passed the motor pool with its tanks, jeeps and trucks. "Look!" he squealed with delight. "They have the whole collection!"

— JEREMY THORNTON

An Army intelligence officer, I took my four-year-old daughter into the office, and before long she spotted a man whose uniform was covered in ribbons, badges and medals. "Is he a general?" my daughter asked. "No, honey," I replied. "He's the first sergeant." With a quizzical look she asked, "Ever?"

— ROBERT H. MILLER

My seven-year-old grandson from New York was in New Orleans visiting when he noticed a photo of me from World War II in a Navy WAVES uniform. He later remarked to my daughter that he was impressed I had served during the war, but was sorry that my side lost. "What do you mean?" my daughter asked. "Well," my grandson replied, "Isn't she from the South?"

— VIOLET Y. WALSH

Our 15-year-old daughter, Melanie, had to write a report for school about World War II, specifically D-Day and the invasion of the Normandy beaches. "Isn't there a movie about that?" she asked me. I told her there was, but that I couldn't think of the name. Then it came to her. "Oh, I remember," she said. "Isn't it something like 'Finding Private Nemo'?"

— REBECCA DEMAURO

While my husband was stationed at Fort Sill, Okla., our children attended a private school. One day my daughter came home with enrollment papers that needed to be filled out for the following school year. "Dad," she announced proudly as she handed over the forms, "here are my re-enlistment papers."

— SANDIE WEBSTER

When I re-enlisted as a Marine, my family came to the ceremony, in which I stood face to face with a lieutenant colonel, our right hands raised. A few weeks later, as I was showing photographs of the big day to my children, my nine-year-old daughter was unimpressed. "Look at Dad," she said. "He thinks he's so cool giving this guy a high-five."

— MICHAEL N. RUSSELL

Parental Pride

I overheard my father telling a family friend about my newly assigned mission in the U.S. Coast Guard. I work on a cutter that escorts all cruise ships and international vessels under the bridges in California's Bay Area. But what my father told his friend was, "She's involved in some sort of an escort service."

— ADRIENNE BLODGETT

As a public-affairs officer in the Air Force, I accompany members of the media while they pursue stories at area bases. But I realized I hadn't explained my job clearly enough to my mother when I overheard her tell a friend, "My daughter provides escort service to television reporters."

— JAMIE S. ROACH

A distraught driver was grateful when our Marine son, Jim, stopped to help put out a fire in her car. "I prayed 'please let the next car stop,' and it was you," the woman gushed. Jim's mother was also pleased when she heard the story. "Who would have thought," she told him, "that you would be the answer to any girl's prayers?"

— RICHARD BELL

When my son, Tom, came home from the Army medical school at Fort Sam Houston on his first leave, I proudly watched him disembark from the plane. He looked so much more mature with his close haircut and immaculate uniform, and I was very impressed that he was carrying a briefcase. I gave Tom a big hug, and, pointing to the briefcase, I asked if he had much studying to do. "No, Dad," Tom replied. "This is my Sony PlayStation!"

— THOMAS W. TOBIN

Family Matters

During the Persian Gulf War, I was assigned to go to Saudi Arabia. As I was saying good-bye to my family, my three-year-old son, Christopher, was holding on to my leg and pleading with me not to leave. "No, Daddy, please don't go!" he kept repeating. We were beginning to make a scene when my wife, desperate to calm him, said, "Let Daddy go and I'll take you to get pizza." Immediately, Christopher loosened his death grip, stepped back and in a calm voice said, "'Bye, Daddy."

— CRAIG S. KUNISHIGE

★ ★ ★ ★ ★ ★ ★ ★ ★ ★ ★

While conducting inspection one morning, I entered the quarters of a young enlisted man. His room was spotless, but I knew something wasn't right. Then I noticed his pants were cuffed, not hanging straight as service regulations demand. "Airman," I snapped, "have you decided to change the Air Force dress code?" "No, sir," he replied. "My mother did. She thought the uniform looked better this way."

— COL. RON COX (RET.)

★ ★ ★ ★ ★ ★ ★ ★ ★ ★ ★

Sixteen years is a long time. That's how far the photo of my husband—looking slim and fit in his Marine Reserve uniform—goes back. Today, he's about 100 pounds heavier, so it was understandable when my friend's son asked who it was. "That's my father," my daughter told him. Looking at my husband, then at the photo, he asked, "Your first father?"

— MELE KOLOKIHAKAUFISI

When my brother, Jarrett, was trying to decide which branch of the military to join, he sought advice from our two uncles, one an Air Force reservist, the other a Marine. After Jarrett had decided on the Corps and left for boot camp, my Air Force uncle told a friend, "I must not be a very good salesman." "I guess not," replied his friend. "But I bet right now you're his favorite uncle."

— AMANDA YOUNG

I was leaving the grocery store with my three young sons when I spotted an Army tank loaded onto a flatbed truck with soldiers standing nearby. Knowing how my boys love anything that has to do with the military, I remarked, "Ooohhh, soldiers!" One of the men gave me a sheepish but somewhat flirtatious grin. Only then did I realize I was standing there alone. My boys had stopped at the gumball machine inside the store.

— TINA COOMES

Soon after we arrived at my husband's new duty station in Groton, Conn., I took our young son to the base hospital to take care of our health records. A Marine

wearing a green, brown and black camouflage uniform, along with heavy combat boots, sat at his keyboard, entering our information. My son stared at him in awe, then turned to me and asked, "Mommy, does he think he's hiding?"

— CAROL KING

At his first parade as a Naval Academy midshipman, my brother, A.J., and the others drilled for hours. Finally, they lined up in columns and were assigned commanders who issued further orders. Many of the mids were anxious and repeatedly made mistakes. But my brother seemed confident and never missed a beat. "Mister," his commander asked, "have you any previous experience?" "Yes, ma'am," A.J. replied. "I have three older sisters!"

— JAYME BARDIN

Service Adjustments

Just after my father, who was a career Air Force NCO, passed away, all my brothers and sisters returned home to be with Mom. As we reminisced about my dad, we found ourselves floating from sorrow to laughter as we brought up fond memories of our nomadic military lifestyle. One morning we were discussing what music should be played at the funeral and several hymns were suggested. "But, Mom," my older sister said, "since Daddy was in the Air Force, shouldn't we request the Air Force song?" "No, dear," my mother said with a smile. "We are not playing a song with the words 'Off we go into the wild blue yonder' at your father's funeral!"

— JOHN H. WILLIAM

★ ★ ★ ★ ★ ★ ★ ★ ★ ★ ★

Some friends were hoping their second child would be a girl, and they even had a name picked out. The ultrasound didn't reveal the baby's sex, though, and since the expectant father had orders from the Navy to ship out before the due date, he told his wife, "We'd better pick out a boy's name, just in case." But when it was time for him to report for duty, they still hadn't decided. At sea a few weeks later, he got notification that his son, Justin Kase, had been born.

— RICH ELKINS

When my husband joined the Coast Guard, I knew there would be some adjustments. Not only did I have to get accustomed to his short haircut, but also to his new sailor lingo. I eventually got used to him saying aye instead of yes, but nothing prepared me for the night when I was seven months pregnant and trying to roll over in bed. In his sleep, with a very military-sounding voice, my husband shouted at the top of his lungs, "She's comin' in on the port side!"

— CHRISTINE BERG

When I worked for the credit union at Fort Sill, Okla., a woman came in twice a month to cash her husband's paycheck, with four boys in tow. The kids didn't misbehave, but they kept their mother busy. One rainy payday, as the woman came with her brood, she dropped a piece of paper. I went over and picked it up for her. "On a day like today," I said, "you should've gotten your husband to take care of this." "Oh, he couldn't," the young mother replied. "He's on vacation in Korea."

— MARI COUCH

★ ★ ★ ★ ★ ★ ★ ★ ★ ★ ★

At a reception following my son Mark's graduation from basic training, he was given the duty of manning a small lemonade stand. A box was placed nearby to collect donations, and a scattering of dollar bills lay at the bottom. After one man put in a $50 bill, Mark sought him out and offered to return the money, convinced the man had put the large bill there by mistake. "Son," the man replied, "my grandson has a job and short hair, and he just called me 'sir.' That's worth fifty bucks any day."

— KATIE NYE

 When you say 'quagmire with no exit strategy,' you're talking about our **relationship,** right?

After our son, Vincent, left for a year's stint with the Air Force in Korea, we decided to send him a string of letters from friends and family taped together to form a banner. Vincent's grandmother had done the same when her brother was in World War II, and she was proud that the banner she'd sent off had measured 18 feet long. My husband and I were determined to match that length, so we feverishly sought out friends and relatives to contribute to the chain. Weeks later we had the banner finished, but it was barely 17 feet long. Still, we sent it off to Korea, happy with our efforts, although a little disappointed that we didn't quite measure up. Shortly afterward my son called to say he had received the banner. "I can't believe how long it is!" he said excitedly. "But why didn't you two write?"

— LOUISE AND RICHARD JONES

When my husband, Bill, was stationed in Germany, our four-year-old son, Darren, would often help me think of gifts to send him. So on learning that Bill would be coming home in late fall, I told Darren we should have a Christmas surprise waiting for him. But I was taken aback by the gift Darren requested for his father from the mall's Santa Claus. "Please, Santa," he asked, "bring me a little brother so we'll have a surprise for Daddy when he comes home."

— JUNE B. SCHUH

> **Sign posted in the Army recruiting office:**
>
> Marry a veteran, girls. He can cook, make beds, sew and is already used to taking orders.
>
> — BRIAN DION

I attended airborne training, where I spent three weeks learning how to pack parachutes and land without hurting myself. I completed five jumps and received my wings. After I returned home, my wife had done a load of laundry and I was helping her fold it. "I can't believe it," she said, after watching me for a while. "You made five jumps with chutes you packed yourself, and you can't even fold a fitted sheet!"

— COL. JAMES T. CURRIE

Love 'em As They Are

A retired Navy admiral, my father began a second career working in a bank. One morning, while he prepared his desk for the day, he was approached by a young officer from the nearby Naval base. "Sorry, but the department isn't open yet," Dad said. "But, it's nine o'clock!" protested the officer. My father didn't look at his watch. Instead, he surveyed his customer's uniform. "Ensign," he snapped, "I'll decide when it's nine o'clock!"

— SUSAN N. BOLINGER

My daughter, then a member of the Oregon Air National Guard, and I were waiting for the driver who would take her to the airport, where she would catch a flight for an overseas assignment. There she stood, punk hair style, three earrings in one ear, bulky sweater, bright red pants, and brass-toed boots. Turning to me, she said, "I'm sure glad they didn't make us wear our uniforms on this trip. I hate to look conspicuous."

— MARY BENTLY-GARDNER

★ ★ ★ ★ ★ ★ ★ ★ ★ ★ ★

On a shopping trip with my daughter, a Navy flight surgeon, I noticed that one item on her list was Snoopy bandages. She said that they were for some of her patients who were unnecessarily upset by their minor scratches and routine shots. Beaming with maternal pride, I told her how thoughtful she was to make the officers' children so happy. "Children?" She said, "Mother, these are for the pilots."

— FRAN SOLOMON SMITH

I spent several years as a submariner, and while at sea we would have a celebration halfway through a patrol. On one such night, the captain, who was serving dinner to the crew, tried to put some vegetables on a recruit's plate. The young seaman wouldn't take them. "With all due respect, sir, " the recruit said, "I don't eat them for my mother, and she outranks you."

— MARK WIDMAN

When I was at Fort Dix, N.J. for Army basic training, my father, an Air Force master sergeant, was stationed at Dover Air Force Base in Delaware. I got a weekend pass, and Dad picked me up Friday evening so we could drive home to Massachusetts. On the way, we stopped at a diner. I was wearing my dress greens and Dad was in dress blues. The waitress looked puzzled as she took our order. "Is something wrong, Ma'am?" I asked. "It's unusual to see men in different services traveling together," she explained. "That's nothing," Dad replied. "He's taking me home to sleep with his mother!"

— DOUGLAS MOORE

When my best friend, James, came home on his first Army leave, my little brother asked him what he did in the service. "I do calisthenics, shoot guns, and follow orders," James replied. Walking in town that day, James and I ran into a buddy who also asked him what he did in the service. James gave the same reply, "I do calisthenics, shoot guns, and follow orders." A while later, we met a former classmate, an attractive woman, and she asked the same question. This time James said, "I'm studying communications, learning foreign languages, and traveling around the world."

— JAMES D. ANGLETON

While we stood at attention during a parade, the private next to me waved to someone in the audience. "Jones, never do that again!" our drill instructor sternly whispered. But a few minutes later, the soldier waved a second time. Back in the barracks after the parade, the DI barreled in and barked for Jones to come front and center. "Son, you knew I was going to see you," he screamed. "You knew it was wrong. Aren't you afraid of me?" "Yes, sir!" replied Jones. "But you don't know my mother!"

— ANDREW G. RAMON

I didn't think I had been gone that long. After 20 months overseas, my ship arrived in San Diego and, as soon as I got ashore, I phoned home. **"Hi, Mom!"** I said. **"Who is this?"** she answered. **"Hello! I'm an only child."**

— JOHN NEDDERMAN

★ ★ ★ ★ ★ ★ ★ ★ ★ ★ ★

I was chatting with a woman about my husband, Marryl, a marine stationed at Parris Island Recruit Training Depot. "What does he do there?" she asked. "He teaches at the drill instructors' school," I replied. She said, puzzled, "I figured they just got the meanest marines they could find and put them to work."

— HOLLY BRISBIN

My husband Brent, our four-month-old baby and I were shopping when Brent remembered he had to take care of some paper work at his army reserve unit. We stopped there near the baby's feeding time, and as we waited for Brent, our little one became increasingly fussy. I sat and rocked him, vainly trying to quiet his cries. Several officers peeked in to check on the commotion. "I know just how he feels," one lieutenant consoled. "I cried my first day in the army, too."

— THERESA MELLOR

I spent my 22nd birthday at the MP school in Fort Gordon, Ga., drilling in the extreme heat. Cleaning up for chow, I was ordered to report to the telegraph center "on the double!" Panting breathlessly after running two miles in the sweltering humidity, I opened the wire that had been sent to me: "HAPPY BIRTHDAY, SON. LOVE, MOM AND DAD."

— ANTHONY ANDRIANO

OOPS!

★ **It's Inevitable**

★ **And So It Goes...**

Two female privates are ordered to paint the general's office. They are warned not to get paint on their uniforms. So they lock the door, strip off their clothes and get to work. An hour later, there's a knock at the door. "Who is it?" they ask. "Blind man." Thinking nothing of it, the privates open up. "Hi," says the man. "Where do you want the blinds?"

— SOURCE UNKNOWN

While serving in the Persian Gulf, I was living in one of the tent cities that housed many of the troops. The tents were pitched so close together that the ropes crisscrossed. As I was heading back from chow, rifle slung over my shoulder, I decided to take a shortcut between the tents. Soldiers living there had hung their laundry on the outstretched ropes, but I deftly ducked under them. As I emerged from this tangle and continued down another pathway, a pair of soldiers pointed and laughed at me. Puzzled, I turned around to find a pair of men's underwear swinging from the muzzle of my rifle.

— KATHY EVANSON

Loading my jeep with a generator, gas and other necessary items for flood victims in Warren, Minn., I drove to a National Guard checkpoint and flashed my fire department badge to get past. The Guardsman waved me through with a picture-perfect salute, and my chest swelled with pride at the show of respect. On my way back out, I stopped to talk to the soldier and thanked him for the salute. "That wasn't a salute, sir," he told me. "I was just showing you how deep the water was."

— PAT COLLINS

While in the field one night on Army maneuvers, my husband, Francisco, came under fire by "opposing" forces. Fortunately, he was using night-vision goggles. Crawling low through the woods, Francisco followed another soldier who was really making time as he moved through the bushes. My husband drew closer to his unusually speedy comrade just in time to realize he was not a soldier at all. Francisco had been trying to keep pace with a porcupine.

— REBECCA LLENAS

On leave after a yearlong tour of duty in Korea, my friend's first craving back home in the States was a meal at McDonald's. Much to his surprise, the cashier took one look at his uniform and refused his money. "Thanks," he said. "Sure," she replied. "We never charge bus drivers."

— LEESA BRAUN

My Air National Guard unit in Virginia Beach, Va., had a change-of-command ceremony, and a high-ranking general came to deliver a speech. He was given VIP treatment and even received some press coverage. The day after the big ceremony, the general took his wife to the movies at a local cinema. When he entered the small theater, he was given a standing ovation. Flattered by the response to his arrival, he acknowledged the applause with a wave of his hand and a big grin. Later, after the movie, one of the patrons approached him. "Gee," remarked the fan, "we are so lucky you came." "Oh, really?" the general replied, obviously pleased. "Yes, they weren't going to start the movie unless they got 15 paying customers. We only had 13 until you two showed up."

— BRADLEY D. STEELE

As new Naval reservists, my friends and I were proud to wear our uniforms to an armed-forces parade in New York City. After leaving the subway, we were walking the short distance to the assembly point when we noticed the green coat, gold buttons and double bars of an approaching officer. We quickly straightened up and presented him with sharp salutes. Our wonder over why the Army captain had not returned our salutes quickly turned to embarrassment when we realized he was a foreman for the New York City sanitation department.

— EDWARD T. ZAREK

On the heels of a massive storm, our supervisor visited headquarters to be briefed. When the major had concluded his rundown, the supervisor pointed to the map, where colored pins indicated affected towns, generators and so on. "What are the red pins at the top for?" he asked. "Those," said the major, "hold up the map."

— MAJ. RYAN JESTIN

During my Army Reserve unit's annual training at Fort Ord, Calif., our battalion commander was upset that evening chow was late. He called the mess hall, and the mess sergeant explained that because their vehicle broke down, they couldn't deliver the field rations to our bivouac site. The commander immediately yelled to his driver, "Private! Drive to the mess hall and get chow!" The private took off on the 15-minute trip. Over an hour later, we were dismayed to see him return empty-handed. "Private!" demanded the commander. "What about chow?" "It was delicious, sir," replied the driver. "I got there right before the mess hall closed, so I got seconds."

— VINCE GILKEY

It's Inevitable!

During Operation Desert Storm, I was a legislative affairs officer for Gen. Norman Schwarzkopf. Often I was required to transport gifts, sent to him from patriotic Americans, from Washington, D.C., to his home base in Florida. On one trip I "escorted" a four-foot teddy bear dressed in fatigues with a name tag reading "Bear," General Schwarzkopf's nickname. As I boarded the plane, I explained my mission to the flight attendant and asked if she could store the bear in first class. She was honored to do so, and I disappeared into the coach section. Then, just before takeoff, an announcement came over the intercom: "Colonel Preast, would you please come up to first class? We have an extra seat here for you to sit next to your teddy bear."

— DAVID R. PREAST

★ ★ ★ ★ ★ ★ ★ ★ ★ ★ ★

During Army basic training, our first lieutenant took us on a march and asked each of us where our home was. After everyone had answered, he sneered and said, "You're all wrong. The Army is now your home." Back at the barracks, he read our evening duties, then asked our first sergeant if he had anything to say. "You bet I do," the sergeant replied. "Men, while you were gone today, I found beds improperly made, clothes not hanging correctly, shoes not shined and footlockers a mess. Where do you think you are? Home?"

— JACK HEAVEY

Jimmy, our son, is an Army ROTC cadet at Northern Arizona University in Flagstaff. During a field exercise, he was assigned to "attack" a designated bunker, but also instructed not to strike if he was outnumbered by more than three soldiers. As Jimmy made his approach, he saw a crowd of people around his target, some in civilian clothes. Since he was vastly outnumbered, he set off a smoke grenade for cover and conducted a by-the-book retreat. Jimmy's captain intercepted him. "Cadet, do you know what you've done?" Unbeknownst to my son, a group of reporters was covering the event. He had just retreated from the press.

— CHUCK BEVAN

> Two green recruits found three hand grenades on the road and decided to take them back to the base. "What if one of them explodes?" asked one young private. "No problem," said his buddy. **"We'll say we only found two."**
>
> — SOURCE UNKNOWN

Our unit stood at attention one morning as the officer in charge presented a shipmate with a Good Conduct Award. The officer read from the certificate, "in recognition of faithful, zealous and obedient naval service." As the certificate was handed over, we heard a voice from the ranks say, "They make it sound like you should wag your tail and bark."

— SUSAN AVILA

"I feel sorry for this soldier," joked my husband as he handed me a flier he'd found in our mailbox. It read: Lost Cat/Black and white/Answers to Nate/Belongs to a soldier/Recently neutered.

— SONDRA GILBERTSON

In the Army during Operation Desert Storm, I found myself in a world that had changed little since Biblical times. With so few creature comforts available, packages from home containing cookies and canned goods were received with great anticipation. When I got a box from my sister, I happily tore into it, only to discover just how far from home I really was. She had filled it with packages of microwave popcorn.

— ROBERT T. SIMS

I was in a Novocain fog following a visit to the dentist when I found myself lost on a deserted highway. Within minutes, I was surrounded by security officers who escorted me home. Later that day, my Air Force pilot husband came home, fuming. "You won't believe what happened!" he said, shaking his head. "Some idiot was driving around the runway and we had to circle until the police could get the car off!"

— PAMELA ISOM

 I'd like to stop saluting, Sir, but my hair is **stuck** in my watchband.

Tiring of the same old buzz cut from the base barber at Fort Dix, New Jersey, I went into town to get my haircut. The hairdresser noticed my accent and asked where I was from. "Trinidad," I said. "Is that in Arabia?" "The Caribbean." She laughed, "I never was good at geometry."
— GERARD D'ORNELLAS

The trip aboard the transport ship that brought my Air Force father and mother to Japan promised to be a long, tedious one. But the Navy, trying to liven things up for the couples, posted this sign by the galley for all to see when they dined: "Officers may mess with their wives between 1100-1200 and 1800-1900."
— LESLIE MATHES

And So It Goes…

When my sister was considering joining the Army, she was showered with attention from recruiters. Cars with drivers were made available to take her to meetings, and every door was opened and held for her. She enjoyed the special treatment and signed up. On the day she left for boot camp, an impeccably dressed sergeant arrived to pick her up. As she got ready to leave, she asked, "Aren't you going to help me with these bags?" "Get them yourself," the man replied. "You're in the Army now!"
— DOROTHY GLENDORA GIBBS

Decal on the door of a military base: "Freedom's Door Is Open to Everyone." Below it, another decal: "Authorized Personnel Only!"
— HEATHER HARRIS

Patrolling the streets of Baghdad is a tense job. But one thing that lightens the mood is sharing treats with the kids. One day, I leaned out of our Humvee and tossed some goodies to the children. I was enjoying the laughter and smiles when I noticed a man glowering at me after some candy landed at his feet. "What's wrong with that guy?" I asked our gunner. "He was pouring cement," he explained.

— JENNIFER TWITCHELL

Nights in England are coal black, making parachute jumps difficult and dangerous. So we attach small lights called chemlites to our jumpsuits to make ourselves visible to the rest of our team. Late one night, lost after a practice jump, we knocked on the door of a small cottage. When a woman answered, she was greeted by the sight of five men festooned in glowing chemlites. "Excuse me," I said. "Can you tell me where we are?" In a thick English accent, the woman replied, "Earth."

— BILL BLACK

I was in the band at Ellsworth Air Force Base, South Dakota. Our group was required to play for all generals who arrived on base. So one morning, when our commanding officer heard on the radio that a General Frost was expected just after noon, he sent us scrambling to the flight line with our instruments. Turns out one of the musicians had also heard the radio announcement. He took the C.O. aside for a whispered conference. When they returned, the officer told us the performance was canceled. There was no arriving general—we had almost played for the weather forecast.

— DAVID YOST

One morning a helicopter crew from my squadron got an order to pick up a mental patient and deliver him to an aircraft carrier. The passenger boarded the copter unescorted, but when it landed on the carrier, four Marines charged in, restrained the bewildered passenger and unceremoniously delivered him to the ship's doctor. Then the flight crew received another message: "Replace mental patient with dental patient." The poor guy had a toothache.

— MICHAEL KVICALA

When my father, a retired Marine, and I were visiting the PX at Camp Lejeune, N.C., we saw his friend, a retired sergeant major, who was continually looking up from his wristwatch. "What are you up to?" my father asked him. "I've been standing here for twenty-eight minutes," his buddy replied, "and not one Marine has come through these doors in full uniform. I'll give fifty dollars to the first Marine who comes in dressed with spit and polish." Within seconds, a private walked into the PX decked out in his full uniform. Pleased, the sergeant major presented him with the money and asked him about his impeccable appearance. The private lowered his eyes and replied, "I've just come from my court-martial, sir."

— TERRY MCGUIRE

During reservists' training, my commanding officer was briefing his colleagues on the battalion's mission. While he was highlighting the key objectives, of our task—serious business, aimed at motivating the troops—he was suddenly interrupted by a ringing cell phone. The tune? "Mission Impossible."

— SAMUEL HENRY

★ ★ ★ ★ ★ ★ ★ ★ ★ ★ ★

There was a high volume of new recruits when I joined the Army. Instead of using our names, we were called by ID numbers. On the second day of reception, a group of new privates awaited instructions. Suddenly a sergeant burst into the room and yelled, "Hey, you, Private!" We all stared, unsure whom he was talking to. Annoyed, the sergeant stepped up to the intended private and shouted, "You!" "Hey," she protested, "I have a number!"

— KAMI HOLLIDAY

During basic training at Lackland AFB in Texas, our flight crew marched back to the barracks after receiving our coveted dress-blue uniforms. Our boots were tied to the duffel bags strapped to our backs. As we marched, one airman called out to the drill instructor, "Sir, permission to adjust. My boots keep kicking me in the butt." "Permission denied," the instructor replied. "Those boots are doing exactly what I've been dying to do since day one!"

— ANTHONY MCCORD

My father, an Army major, was conducting a field test when communications went dead. Immediately, he jumped into a jeep and ordered a sergeant to speed to the command station. When my father and the sergeant ran in, the group there cheered their arrival. The commanding officer then stepped forward and shook my father's hand. "Don't congratulate me, sir," my father said modestly as he pointed to his driver. "It was all the sergeant's doing." The commanding officer nodded and turned to the sergeant. "Congratulations," he said. "The major's wife just had a baby girl."

— DIANE DUDMAN

The HOME FRONT

- ★ Can You Cope?
- ★ We Do Our Best
- ★ It's Really Okay
- ★ Homecoming
- ★ Supportive Spouses?

★ ★ ★ ★ ★ ★ ★ ★ ★ ★ ★

While my husband was stationed overseas, our four-year-old daughter decided that she needed a baby brother. "Good idea," I told her. "But don't you think we should wait till your father's home?" Lori had a better idea. "Why don't we just surprise him?"

— KAY SCHMIDT

Few people know what a quartermaster does. So during my aircraft carrier's Family Day, I demonstrated a procedure called semaphore—I grabbed my flags and signaled an imaginary boat. When finished, I pointed to a little girl in front and asked, "Now do you know what I do?" "Yes," she said. "You're a cheerleader."

— DANNY SULLIVAN

Early in my marriage, I found it hard to get used to the strict rules of Marine life. One time my husband's sergeant suggested he have me wake up at 5:00 A.M., then drive him to another base to pick up a truck they needed. Ashamed to admit it, Steven told his superior that I'd probably be unwilling to help. "She's not a team player, is she?" his sergeant asked. "No," Steven replied. "She's not even a fan."

— KELLY DAVIS KING

> Our son, who's in the Army stationed in Georgia, invited my husband and me for a visit. After driving endlessly through unfamiliar streets in search of an entrance to Fort Stewart, my husband suddenly said, "We're getting close." "How do you know?" I asked. He pointed to a sign that read:
> **"Sonny's Bar-B-Q. Tank Parking Available."**
>
> — WILMA J. FLEMING

★ ★ ★ ★ ★ ★ ★ ★ ★ ★ ★

My family and I had just arrived at a Naval air station in Texas after a tour in Japan. We met another new couple at the base who had been staying in a hotel with their six kids. Since we had already rented a large home, we told them they could stay with us for a few days. "And don't worry about the kids," my wife said. "We have futons for them." "Oh, don't go to any trouble," the wife said. "They eat anything."

— ROBERT J. DOUGHER

As a young married couple, my husband and I lived in a cheap housing complex near the base where he was stationed. Our chief complaint was that the walls were paper-thin and that we had no privacy. This was painfully obvious one morning when my husband was upstairs and I was downstairs on the telephone. I was interrupted by the doorbell and went to greet my neighbor. "Give this to Lieutenant Gridley," he said, thrusting a roll of toilet paper into my hands. "He's been yelling for it for 15 minutes."

— GAIL GRIDLEY

I once lived in Arizona near Fort Huachuca, an Army installation. Our street consisted mainly of mobile homes with small yards, but grass was difficult to grow in that climate, especially with the many children and dogs romping through the neighborhood. One lawn stood out, however. It was green and lush with neat rows of flowers. I was puzzled how the owner managed to do it until I noticed a sign in the yard. It read: "Danger—Minefield."

— ELLEN ZRELAK

★ ★ ★ ★ ★ ★ ★ ★ ★ ★ ★

My brother, Tim, and I were both college students at Texas A & M University, where he was enrolled as a member of the Corps of Cadets, our school's version of ROTC. One day while we were walking through our student center together, I saw an Air Force officer. Noting the eagle on his insignia, I asked Tim, who had not seen the officer, what you call a man with a bird on his shoulder. With a puzzled look, he replied, "A pirate?"

— LINDA EVAN

I had been married for only a week and was just learning about life as a military spouse when I went to the hospital at Randolph Air Force Base near San Antonio for a dental checkup. After the appointment, I took out my checkbook and asked the sergeant behind the counter to whom I should make the check payable. "Honey, this is the military," she said. "We don't take your money, we just take your husband."

— KATHY A. HEDRICK

When faced with overseas duty, I tried to soften the blow of my departure by telling my children we'd be able to buy special things with the extra money I'd earn for the assignment, such as a new car or a vacation. After I'd been in Asia for about six months, I received a tape recording from my children. When my oldest son spoke, he recounted the promise I'd made and then added, "Dad, can you stay a little longer so we can get a new television set, too?"

— LOWELL C. MULLINS

★ ★ ★ ★ ★ ★ ★ ★ ★ ★ ★

My son, a private first class in the Army, was stationed in Bosnia. He called home from his camp one day in good spirits. He said he had just finished a softball game and they didn't even have to chase after the foul balls. "Why not?" I asked. "Because," came a response no mother would want to hear, "the foul line is where the minefield begins."

— KAREN POND

Last Halloween a civilian friend had me pick up his son from day care on the way home from my base. Signing him out, I felt something press against my back. I turned to see him painting on my camouflage uniform. "What are you doing?" I cried. "I like your tree costume," the boy replied innocently. "But you need some red and yellow leaves."

— ADAM CARROLL

Can You Cope?

As a sergeant stationed at Andrews Air Force Base in Washington, D.C., I dated a communications sergeant for the 89th Airlift Wing. Frequently, because of last-minute mission requirements, our personal plans had to be changed. One day before my boyfriend and I were to attend a wedding, I came home to an interesting message on my answering machine: "Ma'am," said a male voice, "this is the Andrews Command Post relaying a message from Sergeant Smith, who is traveling with the Secretary of State. He says he's sorry, but he's out of the country, and so the wedding is off." After a pause, the operator continued in a concerned, unofficial tone, "I hope that's okay, ma'am."

— BARBARA WEBER

★ ★ ★ ★ ★ ★ ★ ★ ★ ★ ★ ★

I was visiting my parents with my new husband, a Navy frogman, when he drew me aside. "I don't think your mother likes me," he said. "I was explaining that I can't wear my wedding ring when I dive because barracudas are attracted to shiny things and might bite off my finger. And she said, 'Well, can't you wear it on a chain around your neck?'"

— MARJORIE MANSON TELFORD

 I can't **heeear you!**

★ ★ ★ ★ ★ ★ ★ ★ ★ ★

According to my mother, she and Dad decided to start a family soon after he became an officer in the Air Force. When months went by without success, they consulted the base physician, who chose to examine Mom right then and there. "Please disrobe," he told her. "With him in the room?" she yelled, pointing to my father. Turning to Dad, the doctor said, "Captain, I think I found the problem."

— WINDLEY HOFLER WALDEN

When my brother, John, joined the Marines about a year ago, friends and family told my mother not to worry, reassuring her that "at least it's during peacetime." On September 11, when terrorists attacked our country, John was stationed in Japan. My mother, upon hearing the news, didn't panic. Instead, she headed to the nearest recruiting office. When a recruiter came to the desk and asked if she needed help, she responded, "Yes—I need to hug a Marine!"

— JULIANNE STARE

My father, an engineer on a submarine, was often out at sea for family occasions. As a result, he sometimes forgot about them. One year he missed my mother's birthday. Unfortunately, it was impossible for her to tell him how furious she was since the Navy screened all messages, editing out anything that could be considered disturbing to the men on board. However, my mother was not so easily defeated. She sent my dad a message, thanking him profusely for the lovely birthday present he so kindly remembered to send her. Mom went on about how special Dad had made her feel by his thoughtfulness, and how grateful she was for his generosity.

— ALEXIS ANDREWS

★ ★ ★ ★ ★ ★ ★ ★ ★ ★ ★

I work on a Navy base in Maryland, across the Patuxent River from my home. When the bridge was closed for repairs, the base provided ferryboats for personnel. After I got to work one morning, my wife, pregnant with twins, called to say that she had forgotten her house key and was locked out. I told her I'd give my key to a sailor working on the ferry, and he could bring it to her at the Navy annex across the river. I explained the situation to a sailor at the marina and told him he'd have no problem recognizing my wife. "She's short, blond and very pregnant," I said. "Buddy," the sailor exclaimed, "this is a Navy base. You'll have to be more specific!"

— PIERRE CONLEY

Marine boot camp was a learning experience for my son. Among the more gruesome skill sets he picked up, he wrote in a letter to the family, was how you can kill a man 12 ways using only your bare hands. This prompted my nephew to wonder aloud, "How does he practice?"

— KELLY SCHACKMAN

A couple of summers ago, our son Scott and his family relocated to Eielson Air Force Base near Fairbanks, Alaska. In awe of the state's wildlife and natural beauty, they looked forward to their four-year tour. That December we received an e-mail from our 11-year-old granddaughter that stated her opinion pretty clearly. It read "Dear Grandma and Grandpa: It is 24 degrees below zero here today. We have three years and eight months left. I love and miss you. Leah."

— BEVERLY BAHNUB

My wife was sitting in the cockpit of my fighter jet—her head spinning as I pointed to the myriad buttons, levers and switches on the control panel. "Do you really know what each one of these buttons does?" she asked. "Yep," I said proudly. Scowling, she then asked, "And I'm supposed to believe you can't figure out how to run the washing machine?"

— MATT DIETZ

Feeling thoroughly sorry for myself after being transferred clear across the continent to Spokane, Washington, I reached out to the one person I knew would sympathize: my mother. "Dear Mom," I wrote, "I have no money and no friends." "Dear Bill," she wrote back. "Make friends."

— WILLIAM SOLOMON

When my father enlisted in the Air Force, he left his church in the capable hands of my mother. Nevertheless, one member of his flock took it upon herself to put Dad's mind at ease. "Pastor, the church is doing well," she wrote. "Your wife is carrying on with the deacons."

— LORA MAE MILLER

During Desert Storm, one of our co-workers was called to serve in Iraq. Upon his safe return and arrival back at work, we tied yellow ribbons around numerous trees and hung a huge sign that read:

"We missed you... thank God the Iraqis did, too!"

— BILLIE MCCRACKEN

★ ★ ★ ★ ★ ★ ★ ★ ★ ★ ★

We Do Our Best

If I say so myself, I looked pretty brawny in my Navy summer whites. And as I stood in line at the Long Beach Naval Hospital pharmacy, I wasn't the only one who thought so—a young boy kept staring at my arms. Eventually, he whispered something to his mother, who, in turn, leaned over to me. "My son wants to know," she said, "if you have a can of spinach in your shirt."

— LOY MCDONALD

After spending a wonderful week together, my fiancé dropped me off at the airport and returned to his base. I didn't realize how much I'd miss him until I reached the plane and burst into tears. "What's the matter?" asked the unlucky woman seated next to me. Between sobs I told her the sad story of my long-distance relationship. "If you truly love him, it will work," she said. "I know. My ex-husband was in the Army."

— ABBY KIESER

As a member of the organization that installs computer systems aboard Navy ships, I am mindful of how important the off-ship e-mail capabilities are to sailor morale, especially when some vessels are deployed for up to six months. One day while shopping at the base commissary, I realized another crucial aspect of my job. I was trailing a frazzled mother with two active children, and I watched as she stalked over to where her young son had perched himself on the rail of the freezer case. "If you don't get off there right now," she commanded, "I'm going to e-mail your father!"

— GREGORY MARTIN

★ ★ ★ ★ ★ ★ ★ ★ ★ ★ ★

It was a very emotional time for me—my youngest son was about to leave for basic training. I took the day off so we could spend his last day as a civilian together. My son likes to pass himself off as a tough guy, but as we climbed into the car, he blurted out in a halting, sad voice, "I'm going to miss you." Well, I just about lost it. The tears flowed from my eyes as I turned to say how much I was going to miss him too. That's when I saw that he was addressing a can of Pepsi he'd just opened.

— SUE STRUTHERS

My husband wore his Army uniform with pride. One day, coming home from the base and dressed in his olive drab fatigues, he stopped off at the grocery store to pick up a few things. While on line at the checkout counter, he noticed a little boy standing with his mother. The boy took one look at my husband in his uniform, and his eyes grew wide. My husband, in turn, gave the young man a crisp salute. The boy was so excited. He pointed at my husband and announced, "Look, Mom, a giant Boy Scout."

— BERNICE QUENTAL

My family wanted to do something to honor my nephew, a Ranger with the Army's 101st Airborne, who had been sent to Iraq. So, with the help of her four-year-old grandson, Chandler, my sister tied a yellow ribbon on the tree in her front yard. "Why are we doing this, Grandma?" Chandler asked. "It's for your uncle," she said. As he watched his grandmother attach the bow, Chandler remarked quietly, "A tree's not much of a present."

— DIANE L. OLWIN

★ ★ ★ ★ ★ ★ ★ ★ ★ ★ ★

During a promotion celebration for my husband, his father, an old Army colonel, introduced himself to the rear admiral in charge by saying, "I've never shaken hands with a rear admiral, and a female rear admiral at that!" He was stunned when she leaned forward and kissed him on the cheek, saying, "Betcha never been kissed by one either!"

— MARIANNE MANN

Reservists like myself always had a hard time parking on base, as most spaces were set aside for the brass. My wife never had this problem. I finally found out why after she drove me to the PX and parked in a space marked "Reserved." "See?" she said. "Just look at all the spaces they've set aside for you Reserves."

— JAMES KLEEMAN

My friend received a package from the Navy containing the civilian clothes her son was wearing when he left for boot camp. Not wanting to open the box, she put it away. This cracked up her husband, who accused her of being a sentimental old fool. "I'm not sentimental," she shot back. "I'm realistic. His shoes, socks and underwear have been inside that box for two weeks, and I'm not going to be the one to open it!"

— SUSAN STUCZYNSKI

★ ★ ★ ★ ★ ★ ★ ★ ★ ★ ★

It's Really Okay

One evening my new husband called to have me pick him up from work. Since I had never been on the military post before, I was a little reluctant, but I agreed to attempt the task. While I drove through the base, a young soldier in his camouflage uniform stepped out onto the street. I slammed on the brakes to avoid hitting him, and the screeching tires attracted the attention of a nearby MP. I was in tears as the officer approached my car. "I didn't see him!" I blurted out. "Well, ma'am," the MP remarked, grinning at me, "that's kind of the point."

— CHRISTIN SMITH

When our son, Jimmy, went to Navy boot camp, we waited impatiently for word from him. Finally we received a postcard telling us he was doing well and we shouldn't worry. It went on to say that he was being kept busy acclimating to a military lifestyle and that he would send a detailed letter in a couple of weeks. After reading his card a second time, however, we noticed that Jimmy had faintly underlined letters throughout the note. When the letters were combined, his hidden message read, "Help me!"

— DONNA GRIMES

Following an overnight flight to meet my father at his latest military assignment, my mother, eight noisy and shoving siblings, and I arrived at Rhein-Main Air Base in Germany. "Do you have any weapons or illegal drugs in your possession?" the customs agent asked my weary mother. "Sir," she said while separating my brother and me, "if I had either of those items, I would have used them by now."

— JIM RISDAL

★ ★ ★ ★ ★ ★ ★ ★ ★ ★ ★

My husband is an Army helicopter pilot, and we never seem to live in one place for very long. Typically, during a move, we stay in a hotel until we can find a permanent place to have our things delivered. Our four children enjoy this greatly, although sometimes it can be a bit confusing for them. One recent day, as we were driving down an interstate and passed a Holiday Inn, our three-year-old squeaked in excitement from the back seat. "Look," he exclaimed. "There's our old house!"

— KIMBERLY O'DONNELL

I was in the perfume aisle of our base exchange and noticed an airman as she picked up a bottle and sniffed its contents. I told her that I particularly liked her selection. "Oh, I'm not buying any perfume," she responded. "When I get homesick for my mom, I always come here to smell her brand of cologne."

— JANE W. RANDO

> I rarely talked to my daughter, Rita, about my military experience, so it surprised me when I overheard her mention it during a phone conversation with her boyfriend. Apparently he was having a hard time adjusting to Army boot camp, and had stolen a moment to call her and complain about his tough regimen. "Look," Rita admonished him, **"if my mother can do it, then you can, too."**
>
> — F. O'GARA

★ ★ ★ ★ ★ ★ ★ ★ ★ ★

My husband's cousin married a former Marine who now works for United Parcel Service. They bought their four-year-old son two stuffed bears—one in a UPS uniform and the other in Marine garb. When the boy seemed confused, his father brought out a picture of himself in full Marine dress. "See, Connor?" he explained, pointing to the photo and then to the bear. "That's Daddy." Connor's eyes went from one to the other, and then he asked in a puzzled voice, "You used to be a bear?"

— ROBIN YEDLOCK

While my brother was stationed overseas, his wife wrote to him daily. For an added touch, she'd always scribble little abbreviated notes on the outside of the envelopes. One day my brother received a letter with the familiar "SWL" (sealed with love) message on the envelope. He noticed that the letter was sealed with tape and chuckled as he read this notation written by a postal employee: "Love didn't stick—resealed in Seattle."

— MARY ANN DAVIS

My friend's wife returned from a tour of duty in the Middle East. To celebrate, he decided to take her out for a night on the town. Proud of her service record, he suggested she wear her uniform. Not only did a patriotic taxi driver refuse to accept money from them, but an appreciative citizen paid for her meal at the restaurant, and the theater manager upgraded their balcony seats to the orchestra. At the end of the evening, my friend turned to his wife. "I still get credit for taking you out, right?"

— JODIE STODDARD

★ ★ ★ ★ ★ ★ ★ ★ ★ ★

Homecoming

After an exhausting military maneuver, our colonel collected his officers and told us, "I intend to go home now, open a bottle of wine and sit with my wife in front of the fireplace. I suggest you all do the same." "Okay, sir," shot back one officer. "If you don't think your wife will mind."

— STEVEN W. CHAPMAN

An Air Force pilot, I was taking a fighter jet from Utah back home to New York, so I called my wife to meet me at the base. Near the end of the flight visibility was poor, and as I began my descent my navigational electronics went dead along with my radio. I managed to find the beacon at the end of the runway and was barely able to make out the ground. Unsure of my situation, the control tower dispatched every emergency vehicle on the base to the runway with lights on and sirens blaring. Fortunately, I landed without incident and taxied to the ramp area. Having seen and heard all the commotion, my wife greeted me with a big hug and said, "Honey, you should have been here for all of the excitement!"

— TOM ROYSTON

After leaving the regulated life of the Navy, an old friend of mine, a retired officer, took a civilian job but had trouble getting to work on time. Finally his boss asked, "What would they have said to you in your previous job about being late?" My friend answered him, "Good morning, Admiral."

— SALVADOR SEPULVEDA, JR.

★ ★ ★ ★ ★ ★ ★ ★ ★ ★ ★ ★

Upon returning from Iraq, I received a number of commendations and medals, including the Bronze Star for meritorious achievement. Still, my daughter was unimpressed. "Who won the Silver and the Gold?" she asked.
— KEITH ANDERSON

★ ★ ★ ★ ★ ★ ★ ★ ★ ★ ★

My neighbor, Terry, a former high-school halfback, came home from combat duty in Afghanistan. He was excited to tell me that his unit had played a makeshift game of football. "Just don't tell my mom," he begged. "If she knew I was playing football she'd worry that I might reinjure my knee."

— MIKE CALLISON

My friend Herb was returning home after several months aboard a Navy submarine. His wife and a crowd of people anxiously awaited the arrival of the vessel at a San Diego dock. She was so excited that she parked their car near the edge of the dock in a no-parking zone. The sub finally appeared. But it came in too fast and slammed into the end of the wharf. Fortunately no one was injured. Unfortunately, Herb and his wife had to explain to their insurance company that their car had been damaged by a runaway submarine.

— DONALD L. HEFLIN

My father was often away on lengthy tours of duty, leaving my mother to manage five kids by herself. While he was away we used to sneak into their room to sleep. So before shipping out one time, Dad reminded us to respect Mom's space and sleep in our own rooms. Upon his return, as he disembarked the plane with the rest of his unit, my brother ran up to him, jumped into his arms and loudly announced, "Dad, you're going to be so happy. While you were gone this time, nobody slept with Mom."

— KATHLEEN HODGE

★ ★ ★ ★ ★ ★ ★ ★ ★ ★ ★

My husband, a war-movie buff, and my six-year-old daughter sat in front of the TV watching actual World War II footage of the unconditional surrender that ended the war with Japan. As General Douglas MacArthur and Japan's General Umeza stood on the deck of the USS *Missouri* and signed documents—under the watchful gaze of Allied troops—my daughter was confused. "What's wrong?" asked my husband. Pointing to the set, she said, "Which one is John Wayne?"

— JENNIE KELLER

My son arrived back in the United States after fighting with the First Marine Division in Iraq. But I still couldn't help reacting like a mom when I saw him on the base running over to some buddies to return a bayonet. "Kevin!" I shouted halfway across the base, before I could stop myself. "Don't run with that knife in your hands!"

— PAM HODGSKIN

I was driving one day when I noticed a car behind me flashing its lights repeatedly. Alarmed, I pulled over, and the other vehicle stopped behind me. Thinking there must be something wrong with my car, I was shocked when an old Army buddy I hadn't seen in 20 years stepped up and shook my hand. We reminisced for a while and then, just before we parted company, I asked him how he knew it was me driving ahead of him. "I marched behind you for years," he said. "I'd recognize the back of your head anywhere!"

— BEN KENT

THE HOME FRONT

★ ★ ★ ★ ★ ★ ★ ★ ★ ★ ★

Supportive Spouses?

Before my husband left for a military-training class one day, he asked me to iron his dress whites for an important inspection the next evening. Having just been married, I ironed the uniform with great zeal, keen to prove my capabilities as a Navy wife and eager for my husband to make a good impression on his superiors. When he came home the following night, he told me that he had passed his inspection and that the commanding officer had said to congratulate me. "Why?" I asked, mystified. "For ironing out the permanent creases that were supposed to be in my uniform!" he replied.

— LYNN MUCICA

Not long ago, a friend in the Army married a woman who was also in the service. The ceremony went splendidly, but my friend's rather domineering mother looked grim throughout the proceedings. At the reception I remarked on this to a major, who also happened to be the couple's commanding officer. "Have you met the bride?" he asked. After I told him I had not, he smiled, drew closer and whispered, "That was no wedding. That was a change-of-command ceremony."

— CHRISTOPHER WIST

Halfway through dinner one night, our friend Jim told us of his days playing football in college as a defensive lineman. "Did you play sports in college, Mike?" his wife then asked me. "Yes," I answered. "I was on West Point's shooting team." "That's great," she said, appropriately impressed. "Offense or defense?"

— MIKE MALONEY

★ ★ ★ ★ ★ ★ ★ ★ ★ ★ ★

One fall, my husband and I attended the San Diego State–Navy football game in San Diego. During halftime I went to a pay phone to check in with my kids but found a sailor in the nearest booth having a teary conversation with his sweetheart. Being a Navy wife, I knew how hard it was being separated from loved ones, so I gladly gave him room for his conversation. My sympathy subsided, however, when I heard his last heartfelt statement: "You know I'd be there with you, honey," he said emotionally, "but I'm stuck here in Virginia."

— TERESA CHRISTENSON

At Fort Riley, Kan., the soldiers' wives were asked to bake treats for a party. My brownies did not turn out well, and I told my husband I would be embarrassed if no one ate them. As a group of soldiers filed in, however, I noticed they bypassed other goodies in favor of mine. I was flattered until I heard one soldier ask my husband, "Hey, Sarge, are these the brownies you told us we better eat, or else?"

— ELIZABETH RADDATZ

Faced with yet another change of bases, I had the unenviable task of packing up our two young children and all our household goods and moving to a new home— without the help of my Air Force husband. One day, after a week of complete chaos as I unpacked and made the other necessary arrangements, I heard the doorbell. When I opened the door, I found a dozen red roses and a small card from my husband. The card said, "Honey, you still move me."

— AUDREY L. MURPHY

★ ★ ★ ★ ★ ★ ★ ★ ★ ★ ★

This one?
That's my **cell phone**.

★ ★ ★ ★ ★ ★ ★ ★ ★ ★ ★

As a sergeant stationed at Fort Meade, Md., I was recommended for a promotion. I had to appear before a promotion board as part of the process, and answer questions about everything from current events to military history. Just when I thought I had successfully completed the interrogation, one first sergeant asked me, "What is the significance of March 9?" My mind raced through the possibilities, but after several tense minutes I gave up and replied, "First Sergeant, I do not know the significance of March 9." "Too bad," he said. "I'm sure your wife would be pleased to hear that you forgot her birthday."

— CWO2 THOMAS M. KANNENBERG

When I entered the Marine Corps, we were authorized to wear only white crewneck T-shirts with our uniforms. While I didn't always keep mine neatly folded and put away, I did separate them by quality. The newest T-shirts were used when I wore my service uniforms, the next best were for wear with utilities or flight suits, and the oldest were for sweaty jobs like mowing the grass. When I got married, my wife began to do my laundry and although she did a much better job, she didn't separate my T-shirts. One day, after I complained that I could not find the "right" T-shirt, I came home to find them neatly folded in three stacks. They were labeled "The Good," "The Bad" and "The Ugly."

— ROY D. BRYANT

★ ★ ★ ★ ★ ★ ★ ★ ★ ★ ★

My husband, Douglas, and I were driving around Luke Air Force Base in Arizona where we had recently been stationed. In front of us was a blue military truck bearing the letters S.W.A.T. and a sign advising people to stay at a safe distance. Suddenly the truck stopped, and several soldiers jumped out. I commented to Douglas that something exciting must have happened—and we were about to witness a dramatic scene. Douglas looked at me and laughed. He explained that S.W.A.T stands for "seeds, weeds and trash." The soldiers were assigned to keep the base clean.

— WENDY MOORE

During our preparation for Operation Desert Storm, I had to make sure the entire crew received immunizations. Our commanding officer, a macho guy, was the most difficult to get to sick bay. He finally showed up late one Friday afternoon. I explained to him that the shots might make him slightly feverish and cranky. "I'll come back on Monday, then," he replied. "Why?" I asked. "Would you rather be irritable to the crew or your wife?" "Doc," he declared, "I'm not afraid of the crew."

— DAVID L. KING

At the completion of our week-long training seminar, 40 of us Naval Reserve chaplains went to Los Angeles International Airport to catch flights home. Dressed in my chaplain uniform, I was walking to the boarding gate when the ticket collector pulled me aside. "I've been watching chaplains get on flights out of Los Angeles all afternoon," she said. "Is something going on that I should know about?"

— WILLIAM W. GASSER

★ ★ ★ ★ ★ ★ ★ ★ ★ ★ ★

Soon after being transferred to a new duty station, my Marine husband called home to tell me he would be late—again. He went on to say that dirty magazines had been discovered in the platoon's quarters and they had to police the area. I launched into a tirade, arguing that many men had pictures hanging in their quarters at our previous post, so his new platoon should not be penalized for something trivial. My husband calmly listened to my gripes and then explained, "Kathy, dirty magazines: the clips from their rifles had not been properly cleaned."

— KATHY ROZINA

As a recruit nearing the completion of basic training at Fort Knox, I was looking forward to my leave home. After 13 weeks of sleeping on the ground, eating army food, and being tormented by drill sergeants, all I could think of was clean sheets, Mom's cooking and some relaxation. Arriving in Boston the day after graduation, I was greeted by my joyous family. "Just wait until you hear about the camping trip we've planned," exclaimed my mother.

— CURT J. CARLSON

Preparing for our wedding, I signed up for dance lessons with my fiancé, an Army sergeant at Fort Meade, Md. We were doing pretty well one day until we got to a complicated turn sequence. My fiancé lost his direction and we both stumbled. "My mistake," my fiancé apologized. **"As you were."**

— A. HICKS

★ ★ ★ ★ ★ ★ ★ ★ ★ ★ ★

My husband's two friends delivered a briefing while taking a course on tactical operations. When they were through, the instructor said the presentation was good, but it had failed to distinguish between engagements and battles. The teacher grew frustrated when no one in the class volunteered to explain that a battle is a series of smaller engagements. "Everyone was responsible for last night's reading assignment," he said. "Surely someone knows the difference." "I know," my husband finally offered. "An engagement is what precedes a wedding, and the battle is what follows."

— KAREN SOTO

I was stationed in Germany as a furniture-supply clerk. My duties included supervising civilian moving crews when an officer changed residences. On one job, a newly promoted Army major general was moving to larger quarters, and, although they weren't my regular men, the crew seemed to be doing well. One fellow, however, carried nothing but small items while the rest lugged the heavy furniture. I informed him in German that if he couldn't carry his fair share, he should sit in the truck and stay out of the way. "Specialist," the general cheerfully replied in English, "that is exactly what my wife told me."

— STEVE RIEPE

LaST LAUGH

★ **The Art of Communication**
★ **Rocks and Other Difficulties**
★ **Respectfully Submitted**
★ **Getting Real**

My unit at Fort Bliss in Texas was detailed with guard duty. However, since live ammunition was reserved for sensitive locations, our rifles were issued with unloaded magazines. One day while we stood at attention for inspection, the officer in charge confronted a private and barked, "What is the maximum effective range of your M-16, soldier?" The hapless private glanced down at his empty rifle and replied, "As far as I can throw it, sir."

— JAN GETTING

After a few rough years, my cousins and their son Jim decided it'd be best if he tried the rigid structure of the military. Since he'd never been one for following rules, we wondered how he'd adjust. It wasn't long before we got our answer. Once he'd completed basic training, he took a two-day drive across the country to his new assignment. Mid-morning on the second day, my cousin was surprised to receive a call from his son, who was still at his hotel. "Why aren't you on the road yet?" he asked. "Well, I'm all ready to go, Dad," Jim replied, "but the sign on the door says, 'Checkout at 11 a.m.'"

— KEN LYNCH

Our air national guard unit conducted weapons-qualifying at the firing range. We had been issued our last round of ammo and were firing at the silhouettes, when a gust of wind ripped the targets from their frames and they fluttered away. Firing stopped as we looked to the range officials. "Keep shooting, boys," a voice yelled. "We've got 'em on the run now!"

— CHRIS B. WITTEK

While stationed at Fort Rucker, Ala., where helicopter pilots are trained, I learned to identify the different copters by their sound alone. Early one morning, I was awakened when one buzzed my barracks. I ran through the possibilities, but couldn't identify it. Intrigued by what kind of helicopter it could be, I sprinted to the window just in time to see the single engine, twin-bladed main rotor lawn mower come into view.

— KAREN BOEHLER

We were using live ammunition during maneuvers in Germany when a phosphorus flare fell short, coming perilously close to me and some of my buddies. We did what most people do under such circumstances—we ran for our lives. "Get back to your weapons!" shouted the officer in charge. "Why are you men running?" As one private ran past him, he answered the officer, "Because we can't fly, sir."

— MYRON EPSTEIN

After completing medical officers basic training, I was assigned to a small Army post in a Boston suburb. I arrived after dark and was directed to my quarters. The next morning a noncommissioned officer escorted me to the commander's office. As we exited the barracks, I looked toward Massachusetts Bay and noticed the back of a large curved device supported by a labyrinth of steel girders. Anxious to impress the NCO with my new knowledge of the Army's air-defense system, I pointed to the structure and said, "So that's our primary target acquisition radar?" "No, sir," the sergeant replied. "That's the back of the drive-in movie screen."

— SOURCE UNKNOWN

A pair of night-vision goggles sets Uncle Sam back a pretty penny. So just before night maneuvers, as my son-in-law handed a pair to a young private with a reputation for losing things, he warned, "Hold on to these!" Afterward, my son-in-law ran into the private, who said, "I have good news and bad news." "You lost those goggles?" "No, of course not." "So what's the bad news?" "I lost the Humvee."

— CONNIE STACY

The Art of Communication

As a department head stationed on a Navy vessel, I was concerned about one of my senior enlisted men. He was a superb technician, but he had a problem taking orders. One day I took him aside and suggested he try something that had worked for me. "Whenever an officer gives you a directive that you think is stupid," I told him, "just say, 'Yes, sir.' But in your mind, think, 'You're an idiot!' Will this work for you?" He smiled at me and replied, "Yes, sir!"

— LEO KING

My thick Southern accent is often a source of miscommunication. One night while driving through base housing, I saw four skunks crossing the road. The next day I told my supervisor what I saw. "So did you get Tom Hanks' autograph?" he asked. "Excuse me?" I said, puzzled. "Didn't you say you saw Forrest Gump in base housing last night?"

— ERIC GRUBBS

The base's public-address system is the simplest way to call the troops—just shout out the soldiers' last names, tell them where they're needed, and they'll hustle right over. But there was some head-turning the day I summoned these two privates to assist the chaplain: "Pope, Paul, please report to the orderly room."

— GREG KNOBLOCK

My wife, Dolores, never quite got the hang of the 24-hour military clock. One day she called the orderly room and asked to speak with me. The person who answered told her to call me at the extension in the band rehearsal hall. "He can be reached at 4700, ma'am," the soldier advised. With a sigh of exasperation, my wife responded, "And just what time is that?"

— ERIC D. ERICKSON

One night at McChord Air Force Base in Washington, I was dispatched to check out the security fence where an alarm had gone off. The fence was at the end of the base runway. When I got to the scene, I found that a raccoon was the culprit, so I ran around and flapped my arms to scare off the animal. Suddenly an air-traffic controller came over the public-address system and announced loudly, "Attention to the airman at the end of the runway. You are cleared for takeoff."

— CHAD BLAKE

As his destroyer entered fabled Pearl Harbor, my friend stood alongside a cocky lieutenant and the Hawaiian harbor pilot. "So tell me," said the lieutenant to the pilot, "is your state pronounced 'Huh-WI-ee' or 'Huh-VI-ee'?" "We say 'Huh-VI-ee,'" the pilot answered. "And that sign over there," asked the lieutenant, pointing ashore, "is it pronounced 'Pi-Pee-Lie-Nee'?" "You could say it that way," said the pilot. "But we Huh-VI-ans usually just say 'Pipeline.'"

— BRUCE CLARK

My helicopter aircrew was into its seventh hour of flying replenishment missions to Navy battle groups off the coast of Sicily when we approached a ship for landing, only to be told we had to circle overhead. Just as I was beginning to get nervous because we were running low on fuel, my crew chief asked me to fly down and hover alongside the ship's bridge. I obliged and I could see the captain of the ship look at us, then frantically pick up the phone. Within seconds we were given clearance to land. "What did you do?" I asked the crew chief, amazed. "Not much," he answered nonchalantly. "I just held their mailbag out the door."

— KIM SHELDON

★ ★ ★ ★ ★ ★ ★ ★ ★ ★ ★

Rocks and Other Difficulties

My parents scoffed, but I knew my college degree in geology would come in handy one day. It was during basic training, at Sheppard Field, Texas, and I was pulling KP duty. When the sergeant asked me what I did in civilian life, I proudly announced that I was a geologist. "Good. I'm looking for someone with your background," he said, while dropping a bulging sack onto the table. "You've got just the right qualifications to pick the rocks out of this hundred pounds of beans."

— RALPH NICHOLS

While a friend and I were visiting at Annapolis, we noticed there were several students on their hands and knees assessing the courtyard with pencils and clipboards in hand. "What are they doing?" I asked our tour guide. "Each year," he replied with a grin, "the upperclassmen ask the freshmen how many bricks it took to finish this courtyard." "So what's the answer?" my friend asked him when we were out of earshot of the freshmen. The guide replied simply, "One."

— GREGORY BOKENKAMP

While stationed with the Strategic Air Command, I found a memo typed on official letterhead. At the bottom of the letterhead was our motto: "Peace is our profession." Beneath that, someone had added: "Bombing is only a hobby."

— DAVID FRENCH

LAST LAUGH ★

 **Don't worry, these sand storms never last more than an hour.**

Out of the Navy and ready to buy my own home, I filled out the veterans loan forms and mailed them away. But what I didn't realize was that I had placed the forms in the envelope containing a lock of hair from my two-year-old son's first haircut. Two weeks later I received this note: "Enclosed is your loan certificate. Regardless of what you were told, we really don't need a sample of your DNA."

— FRANCIS T. JIMMIS

The first thing I noticed when I picked up my clothes from the off-base laundry was that they reeked. So the next week, I sent my clothes over with a note complaining, "My laundry had a peculiar musty odor when I got it back." When my clothes were returned, I found the following appended to my note: "How do you think it smelled when we got it?"

— ROBERT EDDY

When I was stationed in Würzburg, Germany, I ran several miles every day along the beautiful Main River. Once, several fellow lieutenants, all men, joined me. For the first half of the run I was able to keep up with them. However, on the return I started to fall behind. "How are you doing back there?" one of the guys called. "Fine," I replied. I didn't want to admit I couldn't keep up with their fast pace, so looking past the river to the vineyard-covered hills, I said, "I'm just enjoying the view." One lieutenant, running easily in his skimpy nylon shorts, hollered back, "Thanks!"

— VIRGINIA B. TAYLOR

When my Navy Medical Reserve Unit was called up for Operation Desert Storm, I was awakened by a phone call at three o'clock on a Sunday morning with the order to report for duty in four hours for processing. After I hung up the phone, my husband groggily asked, "Who was that?" "Oh, honey," I moaned, thinking of our 15-month-old child, "I have to go to war!" "Don't worry," he said as he rolled over, "It's Sunday, and the traffic won't be bad."

— LINDA P. DEMARCHE

My former boyfriend, Duncan, was an officer in the Naval Reserve. One day while stopped at a red light, his car was rear-ended. As the other driver, a sailor, approached, his eyes widened when he saw the lieutenant's uniform. "It gets even better," Duncan said with a smirk. "I'm also a lawyer."

— BATYAH CHLIEK

Friends of ours were driving along the road one day when they collided with a camouflaged Army truck. Everyone was okay, but when asked by the soldiers what had happened, our friends told them, "We just never saw you coming."

— ANGIE MANSFIELD

Aboard the USS *Tarawa* for six months, my brother, Don, posted a picture of his beloved truck in his locker. Since his fellow Marines had pictures of their girlfriends up, they often ridiculed him for his object of adoration. "Laugh all you want," Don told them. "At least my truck will still be there when I get home!"

— SHERRY TOMBOC

As I guided an elderly safety inspector on a trip around an oil rig out at sea, I invited him to take the helm. "Turn to port," I said, adding, "that's left to you. Now, turn starboard—that means right." Having circled the rig, I joked, "Now, give the boat back to the driver." As he did so, I asked him about his career. "Navy," he said. "Twenty years. Submarines." Then he leaned in. "I was the driver."
— BRUCE MILLAR

Respectfully Submitted

I was sending out military recruitment pitches when I found one addressed to a guy named "Lord." When I filled in the form letter, it read, thanks to some strange computer glitch, "Dear Lord, I need to speak to you as soon as possible regarding your service to your country." I laughed and mailed it off. Weeks later, the letter was returned with a note: "The Lord doesn't live here. If you find his address, let me know. I also need to speak with him."
— MATTHEW WELDY

During basic training, our drill sergeant asked all Jewish personnel to make themselves known. Six of us tentatively raised our hands. Much to our relief, we were given the day off for Rosh Hashanah. A few days later, in anticipation of Yom Kippur, the sergeant again asked for all Jewish personnel to identify themselves. This time, every soldier raised his hand. "Only those who were Jewish last week can be Jewish this week," declared the sergeant.
— ALLEN ISRAEL

I was on board the USS *Kitty Hawk* when we docked in the Sri Lankan capital, Colombo. One morning, as the local fishing fleet passed by on its way out to sea, a boat came too close to our ship. A Marine held up a sign warning the captain to stay away, and he complied. But the next day, the boat was back. This time, the fisherman held something. The nervous Marine pointed to his rifle. The fisherman lifted the object and unfurled it, revealing a sign of his own. In perfect English it read "Your Sign Is Upside Down."

— KEVIN MELIA

The sweat dripping off my brow gave away my secret: I dreaded giving blood. "This'll only take 15 minutes," said the nurse on our base. Pointing to a judge advocate general also donating a pint, I said, "She's been here longer than that." Another donor interjected, "That's because she's used to taking blood, not giving it."

— NATE SMITH

Our bomb squad commander at Fort Lewis, Washington, was testifying in court about a traffic accident. When the prosecutor began questioning her, the captain suddenly lost her voice. "I'm sorry," she said to the judge. "I guess I'm nervous." "You're nervous?" laughed the judge. **"And what exactly is it you do again?"**

— LT. DIANA MANCIA

Although I knew our commanding officer hated doling out weekend passes, I thought I had a good reason. "My wife is pregnant and I want to be with her," I told the CO. Much to my surprise, he said, albeit curtly, "Permission granted." Inspired by my success, a fellow soldier also requested a weekend pass. His wife wasn't pregnant. So when the CO asked why he should grant him permission, my friend responded, "My wife is getting pregnant this weekend and I want to be with her."

— DOUG LADLE

My father, a retired Air Force pilot, often sprinkles his conversation with aviation jargon. I didn't realize what flying had meant to him, however, until the day he showed me the folder with his last will and testament. It was labeled "Cleared for departure."

— CHERYL E. DRAKE

As the commander made his way up front to speak, tension was high. Plans to move the Camp Lejeune Marines north for cold-weather exercises could all be for naught. "General," an officer spoke up, "there's no snow in the forecast." The general called out to a member of his battle staff. "Chaplain, I believe that's your department." "With all due respect, sir," said the chaplain, "I'm in sales, not production."

— BO RUSSELL

★ ★ ★ ★ ★ ★ ★ ★ ★ ★ ★

Getting Real

Some people are extremely impressed when you tell them you're a Navy SEAL. Case in point: my grandson's pre-kindergarten class. It was career day, and I was regaling them with stories of my exploits in the military. After I finished, hands shot up in the air. The kids were fascinated and eager to ask questions. "So," asked one little girl, "can you balance a ball on your nose?"

— G.A. DAVIS

I was working at the base exchange one busy day when the line grew quite long. There was much grumbling among those waiting, but one man made light of the situation. He approached a woman who was obviously very pregnant and tapped her on the shoulder. "Would you mind my asking a personal question?" he said. "Were you pregnant when you got in this line?"

— JAN BOILEAU

My father, an Air Force Academy graduate, still retains a strict military code of ethics as well as a quick wit. One day I mentioned that I was thinking about getting my belly-button pierced. "No way!" my father fired back. "This is an Air Force family—no navel destroyers are allowed!"

— SARAH BLOMQUIST

On the wall of the mess hall of one Marine Corps base:
**"This food must be good.
Ten thousand flies can't be wrong!"**

— JOE TURMAN

I was golfing with a soldier who had just returned from Afghanistan. His plans included becoming a greens keeper once he was discharged in a few months. He applied to a local college for its golf course superintendent program, but the department chair worried that he might not be up for the job. "It's stressful," he said. "You have to fight the weather, insects and demanding club members." "Will anyone be shooting at me while I mow the grass?" asked the soldier. "Of course not." "I'll take the job."
— BILL BAILEY

Upon retiring from the service, my husband, Don, needed a new ID card showing he had gone from active duty to retirement status. But the photo taken of him was not particularly good. And he wasn't at all quiet about it. "If I have to carry that ID around with me for the rest of my life," he complained to the photographer, "I want a better picture!" "Want a better picture?" asked the photographer defiantly. "Then bring a better face."
— NANCY WALLIS

Flying into a Middle East Airport, my copilot and I reviewed our flight plan for the trip back to the USS *Enterprise*. We were to pick up a Navy captain, and experience had taught me that even seasoned vets turn white-knuckled during carrier landings. Once the captain was strapped in, I turned around to welcome him on board. "Sir," I asked, "will this be your first carrier landing?" Looking at me with disdain, he opened his inflatable vest to display gold wings above five rows of ribbons. "Son," he said, "I have over 500 carrier landings in jet fighters." "That's good to hear," my copilot said, winking at me, "because this will be our first."
— KENNETH J. TONELLI

I recently returned to work after a year abroad with the Army Reserve. On my first day back, a visitor from headquarters took me aside. "How are you?" he asked, looking concerned. "Do you feel all right?" "I'm fine," I replied, nonplussed. "Great!" he said. "I heard that you were away from work for a year because you were in a wreck." It took a minute before it dawned on me what he meant. "Iraq," I said finally. "I've just come back from I-raq."

— DEREK SCHNEIDER

Eager to speak military English the way the pros do? Then remember this simple rule—the most basic word comes first. For example: Trousers, Green, Male; Truck, Cargo, 4x4. On a recent trip to the Air Force Academy commissary, I saw, written on the side of a large carton, yet another example: Melon, Water.

— JOSEPH R. SIMKINS

My office collects care packages of snack food and reading materials to be sent to the Army Reserve stationed in the Middle East. Among the suggestions for gifts was rat poison, apparently to deal with a persistent problem in their housing units. "That's a first," I said to my coworkers. "Now we're sending packages to Afghanistan containing weapons of mouse destruction."

— JOHN ALBRIGHT

At the canteen on base, we sold snacks, coffee and soda for 25 cents. One night, we decided to charge officers 50 cents. It was explained away as a "Sir charge."

— ROBERT P. THORNE

★ ★ ★ ★ ★ ★ ★ ★ ★ ★ ★

In the Navy much of our time is spent at sea, drilling for emergencies. Once when our ship was conducting simulated combat exercises, a message came over the loudspeaker: "This is a drill, torpedo hit to starboard, all hands prepare to abandon ship—land bears 090 degrees, 11 miles. Running to my abandon-ship station, I was stopped by a young seaman, apparently on his first sea tour. "Excuse me," he drawled, "but if we really had to swim for it, how would we deal with those bears?"

— RANDOLPH HERROLD

Our new commander was the gung-ho type, determined to shake things up on the base. No detail was too small, not even the IN and OUT trays on his desk. "Get rid of them," he told me. "I don't want them on my desk." As the supply sergeant, I knew that the company clerks relied on those trays to process work. So I offered him an alternative, which he liked. After that, one tray read CHALLENGES and the other CONQUESTS.

— ALAN ANDERSON

Like many American soldiers stationed in Saudi Arabia, I had my picture taken as I sat on a camel. I figured it would be a good souvenir to send home. A few days later, some buddies and I were visiting a local town. When we returned to our vehicle, we found two young Saudis taking each other's picture—sitting on our jeep.

— TOBIE W. JOHNSON

I didn't realize how deep the inter-service rivalry between the Navy and the Marine Corps ran until just before my son's birth. At a prenatal checkup, I asked my obstetrician, a Navy officer, what type of anesthesia he was planning to use. "You're a marine officer's wife, aren't you?" he said. "Yes," I answered. "Well, then," he replied, "You get to bite on a silver bullet."

— DALE EMKEN

ON the JOB

★ **From the Mess**
★ **In Flight**

While my son, Cliff, was on board the Navy carrier USS *George Washington,* the air wing was busy with training missions. After talking to a pilot, one air-traffic controller accidentally left his microphone on and remarked to a nearby buddy, "That guy sounded just like Elmer Fudd." The airwaves got strangely quiet as everyone listening realized the pilot had also heard the comment. After about ten seconds, the pilot broke the silence by announcing, "Be vewy, vewy quiet. We are hunting submawenes."

— WAYNE ROBERTSON

Life on board an aircraft carrier is noisy, with jets, mechanical equipment and the dull roar of blowers circulating air. One night the ship had a massive power failure, and our berthing compartment became abruptly quiet. Everyone woke up with a start. One half-asleep seaman shouted, "What the heck was that!" From across the dark room came a voice, "That was silence, you idiot!"

— JAMES TODHUNTER

My job on our combat store ship was to make sure that the 21 three-ton forklifts on board were firmly secured and positioned to keep the ship on an even keel. One night I was told to report to the captain's stateroom. After I knocked and entered, the captain silently folded his arms, lifted his feet, then pushed himself away from his desk on his chair, which was equipped with wheels. He slowly coasted across the room to the starboard side, then said, "Dismissed." I took the hint and moved six forklifts to the port side.

— RICHARD E. KOONS

Doing tech support for the Navy, my husband is used to dealing with frustrated clients. So when a woman proceeded to spit out every curse word she'd ever heard, it didn't faze Craig. Eventually she calmed down. "Pardon my French," she said. Craig was sympathetic. "I've worked here a long time," he said, "and the one thing I've noticed about the Navy is that everyone is fluent in French."

— JENNIE PAGE

I was serving on a destroyer when we passed an old frigate off the coast of Bermuda. Looking through my binoculars, I was startled to see that the other ship was drifting into our path. Clearly it had come untethered from its anchor. I alerted my captain, who immediately contacted the frigate. "Have you lost your anchor?" he asked. The other captain responded, "No, sir. I know exactly where it is. It's five miles back."

— R. J. M. HARDY

While scrubbing the decks of our Coast Guard cutter on a scorching summer day, a few shipmates and I decided to break the rules and go for a swim. With no officers in sight, I scrambled atop a railing 40 feet above the water. Just as I leaned forward, I could see the captain step out on the bridge. Too late to stop, I did a picture-perfect dive into the ocean. When I had clambered back aboard, the captain was there to greet me. Fearing the worst, I was greatly relieved when he said, "I'll give you a ten." "Thanks, Captain," I said. "I used to dive in college." "I don't mean a score of ten," he spat back. "I mean ten days of restriction."

— RUSTY JACKSON

★ ★ ★ ★ ★ ★ ★ ★ ★ ★ ★

The crew of a fast frigate was practicing the man overboard drill by "rescuing" a bright orange fluorescent dummy dubbed Oscar. The captain watched as a young lieutenant nervously stopped the ship, turned it and maneuvered into place. Unfortunately, he ran right over Oscar. Surveying the remains of Oscar scattered around the ship, the captain told the lieutenant, "Son, do me a favor. If I ever fall overboard, just drop anchor and I'll swim to you."

— ANTHONY WATSON

We were on our destroyer's bridge when the captain noticed something wrong with our course. "I believe you're out of position," he told the junior officer. "Please come to the left a little." So the officer took a step to the left. "I don't think that's far enough," said the captain. So the officer stepped left again. "Perfect," the captain said. "Now bring the ship with you."

— FRANK COLLINS

The commander of the C-141 was in a hurry to fly out of the U.S. air base in Thule, Greenland. But everything was working against him. The truck to pump the sewage from the plane was late, and then the airman pumping out the tank was taking his time. The commander berated the lowly airman, threatening to have him punished. Turning to the officer, the airman said, "I have no stripes, it's 40 degrees below zero, I'm stationed in Thule, and I'm pumping sewage out of airplanes. Just how do you plan on punishing me?"

— JAMES STILWELL

My daughter, Michelle, is the commander of a Coast Guard cutter. When she gave my husband, Bob, a tour of her ship, he was impressed with the neatness of all decks. However, when Michelle brought Bob to her house, he couldn't believe the disorganization. "Why is everything in its place on your ship," he asked, "but your house is such a mess?" Michelle replied, "My house doesn't take 30-degree rolls."

— MARY ANN SCHALLIP

Dead ahead, through the pitch-black night, the captain sees a light on a collision course with his ship. He sends a signal: "Change your course ten degrees east." "Change yours ten degrees west," comes the reply. The captain responds, "I'm a United States Navy captain! Change your course, sir!" "I'm a seaman second class," the next message reads. "Change your course, sir." The captain is furious. "I'm a battleship! I'm not changing course!" "I'm a lighthouse. Your call."

— SOURCE UNKNOWN

As a retired Air Force officer vacationing in Florida, I was playing a round of golf at Pensacola Naval Air Station with three Navy officers. I marveled at the splendid course, which included a tall white stake placed in each fairway to mark 150 yards to the green. At first I feared these markers would be distracting, but I soon found they helped me aim my shots. I mentioned to my companions that distance indicators at Air Force golf courses are flush to the ground, along the edges of the fairway. "Well," one of my Navy friends remarked, "sailors play their best when they can see a mast on the horizon."

— STEVE FISH

★ ★ ★ ★ ★ ★ ★ ★ ★ ★

A shore-based officer, I had the opportunity to go aboard a Navy vessel for a week of training. On the first day we were pivoting into a slip on the pier, and the commanding officer patiently explained a variety of technical terms. Wanting to increase my shipboard vocabulary, I commented on the way we were pulling into port and asked the CO if there was a term to describe our maneuver. "Yes," he answered. "We call it 'backing up.'"

— TANYA L. WALLACE

While on patrol with the Coast Guard, we stopped to help a sailor whose boat was hung up on a sandbar. I asked the owner what had happened. He gave us a lengthy description of his boating experience, then explained that his navigational chart failed to show the sandbar. Skeptical, I asked to see the chart. It was actually a place mat from a seafood restaurant.

— LANCE HANNA

The seas were rough the day the transport ship carried us to Europe. As we pitched up and down, there wasn't one soldier onboard who didn't feel seasick. To take our minds off the bleak conditions, we were invited to see a movie. What film did the captain choose to calm our frayed nerves? *The Caine Mutiny*.

— ROGER COBURN

As a seaman aboard an aircraft carrier, it was my duty to make the morning coffee for my department. After a year of this, I felt a rush of relief when, on the day before my promotion, my department chief put his arm around my shoulder and said, "Rhodes, this will be the last day you'll

be making coffee as a seaman." My heart sank, however, when he added, "Tomorrow will be your first day making it as a petty officer."

— JOHN R. RHODES

After spending a few years on shore duty, I found myself back at sea trying to remember what all of the signal bells and whistles piped over the ship's intercom meant. I was beginning to catch on again when I heard an unfamiliar beeping in the chief's mess. "What's that one?" I asked. When my coworkers finally stopped laughing, they informed me it was the microwave.

— MELANIE M. PATTERSON

 **Don't worry, ma'am. He left a trail.**

★ ★ ★ ★ ★ ★ ★ ★ ★ ★ ★

From the Mess

Once a week we were served steak at my base's mess hall. The meat was so tough you could hardly chew it. When we complained to our colonel, he agreed to come to dinner with us to see for himself. Sure enough, the steak was tough as usual, but after the meal the colonel said nothing. A few days later he sent a memo to the sergeant in charge of the mess. It read: "Sharpen all knives immediately."

— JOHN G. DAVIS

I wanted to make my mark as the new food-service officer at a recruit training center. The menu was loaded with red meat, so I devised a new one to reduce cholesterol. I substituted chicken for beef, and awaited comments from the suggestion box. The first one summed up the recruits' feelings. It read simply, "Let the chickens live."

— RAWLINS LOWNDES

Soon after our son's ship returned to base after a six-month deployment, friends and family of the crew were given permission to tour the vessel. Lunch was served in the mess, and since I had never eaten Navy food, I decided to try a little taste of everything. As I approached some soggy-looking spinach, I pointed out to the sailor standing behind the counter, "There's no serving spoon in the spinach." "Ma'am," he responded quite apologetically, "no one's ever asked for the spinach before."

— PATRICIA K. DOYLE

I was dishing out chow to the Marines at Cherry Point, North Carolina, when an irate gunnery sergeant slammed his tray on the counter and pointed to a cooked grasshopper sitting on top of his spinach. "Look at that!" he barked. Motioning to the other Marines waiting in line, my boss, the mess sergeant, leaned over. "Keep it down, Sarge," he whispered, "or else they'll all want one."

— RON PIRKLE

"Chow looks wonderful," I told the mess sergeant, a large, intimidating man. "I'd love seconds." "You'll get the same as everyone else," he growled as he chucked food on my tray. "Now move it!" After finishing the edible portion of my meal, I dumped the rest in the garbage, accidentally tossing out my silverware. While leaning into the trash can to look for my knife and fork, I felt a tap on my shoulder. It was the mess sergeant. "It's all right, son," he said. "You can grab seconds."

— SCOTT POPE

A sign posted on the wall of an Army mess hall read: "Don't Waste Food—Food Will Win the War."
Beneath these words someone had scrawled:
"That's fine, but how do we get the enemy to eat here?"

— IRVING SCHIFF

While dining in the officers club at an air base in the Philippines, my wife and I lost our appetites when a rat scurried past us. "Waiter!" I said, pointing to the rodent. "What are you going to do about that?" "It's all right, sir," he said unfazed. "I've already confirmed he's a club member."

— KIRBY HUNOLT

I am a grocer's nightmare. I pinch and squeeze each piece of fruit before making my choice. One day, at the base commissary, I was in my element, manhandling all the melons before finally settling on a perfect specimen. "Excuse me," I heard, as I started for the tomatoes. It was my husband's commanding officer. "Mind showing me which one was your second choice?"

— JACKI KECK

Distrustful of Army chefs' culinary talents, my father quizzed the top cook at his base. How did he know when the food was ready to be served? Dad asked. "Easy," said the sergeant, glaring back.

"When it's burning, it's cooking. When it's smoking, it's done."

— BRIAN HENDRICKS

★ ★ ★ ★ ★ ★ ★ ★ ★ ★ ★

In Flight

As he reviewed pilot crash reports, my Air Force military science professor stumbled upon this understated entry: "After catastrophic engine failure, I landed long. As I had no power, the landing gear failed to deploy and no braking was available. I bounced over the stone wall at the end of the runway, struck the trailer of a truck while crossing the perimeter road, crashed through the guardrail, grazed a large pine tree, ran over a tractor parked in the adjacent field, and hit another tree. Then I lost control."

— JOHN D. MILLARD

My uncle was a flight surgeon in the Air Force Reserve. Part of his training included practice runs with jet-fighter pilots. Sometimes they would have fun at his expense, performing aerial maneuvers in an attempt to make him sick. In the middle of one hair-raising turn, the pilot asked him how he was handling all of the flips and twists. "I'm fine," replied my uncle calmly. "Just don't forget, your physical is tomorrow."

— DREW SMITH

I was proud and excited on my first day of Air Force pilot training as I walked toward the instruction facility. From a distance I could see large letters looming over the entrance: "Through these doors pass the best pilots in the world." My pride was quickly deflated, however, as I reached the threshold and read the small, scribbled cardboard sign that had been taped to the glass by a maintenance worker. It said "Please use other door."

— JAMES BIERYLA

Military guys can't help debating which branch is the best. A friend was asked why he chose the Air Force over the Navy. "Simple, really," he said. "Whatever goes up must come down. But whatever goes down doesn't necessarily have to come up."

— JESSE DAVIS

Riding in a jet trainer for the first time was exhilarating. It was also frightening, especially when I began to think, What if we crash? "Excuse me," I said to the pilot. "Is there anything I should know in case we need to eject?" "Yes," he said. "If I say 'Go' and you say 'What?' you'll be talking to yourself."

— HARRY FOSTER

Listening to a lecture about jumping out of airplanes in an emergency made my son-in-law's classmate uneasy. "We only get one parachute?" he asked the instructor. "Where's our reserve?" "Son, you're a pilot. You're supposed to land the airplane," came the answer. "That means the parachute is your reserve."

— BARBARA GRAYDON

The topic of the day at Army Airborne School was what you should do if your parachute malfunctions. We had just gotten to the part about reserve parachutes when another student raised his hand. "If the main parachute malfunctions," he asked, "how long do we have to deploy the reserve?" Looking the trooper square in the face, the instructor replied, "The rest of your life."

— KENNETH RAUENS

★ ★ ★ ★ ★ ★ ★ ★ ★ ★ ★

My boyfriend, Tim, a mechanic, does work for the Air Force Academy. One day, a guard asked, "Mind if our new guard dog practices sniffing your truck?" Tim obliged and the dog went to work. Almost immediately, it latched onto a scent and jumped into the truck bed, sniffing furiously. Tim grew nervous. There were no drugs, no weapons. What could the dog be after? A few minutes later, the guard approached Tim. "Sorry," he said sheepishly. "Our dog ate your lunch."

— CHRISTI LIGHTCAP

The team of guys who packed our parachutes at Bitburg Air Base in Germany were a proud and cocky bunch. So much so, they posted this sign outside their shop: Depend on Us to Let You Down.

— STEVE JURACKA

After enlisting in the 82nd Airborne Division, I eagerly asked my recruiter what I could expect from jump school. "It's three weeks long," he said. "What else?" I asked. "The first week they separate the men from the boys," he said. "The second week, they separate the men from the fools." "And the third week?" I asked. "The third week, the fools jump."

— ROBERT GARDINIER

One of my first assignments for my college newspaper was to cover weekend maneuvers with the Air Force ROTC. When I boarded an ancient C-119 cargo plane for a training flight—my first time ever on a plane—a gruff sergeant strapped me into a parachute. "What do I do with this?" I asked nervously. "If we're going down," he said, "jump out of the plane and pull the rip cord." "When do I pull the rip cord?" I yelled as he walked away. "Before you hit the ground," he called back.

— JOHN H. STENGER

Following a few frantic minutes, air-traffic controllers finally made radio contact with the lost young pilot. "What was your last known position?" they asked. "When I was No. 1 for takeoff," came the reply.

— PHYLLIS NIELSON

During the second Gulf War, I was an Air Force colonel. I routinely flew on different aircraft to familiarize myself with their capabilities. One day I was aboard an intelligence aircraft where each crew member was surrounded by complex gear. A young major showed me his computer screen. "That's a chat screen, sir," the soldier said. "We use it to relay enemy information to the crew—like instant messaging." Nodding, I moved down the line. Flashing on an airman's screen several feet away was the warning: "Heads up—the colonel is on his way!"

— JAMES MOSCHGAT

> What's the difference between a fighter pilot and a jet engine?
>
> **A jet engine stops whining when the plane shuts down.**
>
> — SOURCE UNKNOWN

One month into Marine Corps training in San Diego, Calif., we were preparing for a ten-mile march in 100-degree weather when a jeep drove up with a large radio in the back. "Who knows anything about radios?" our drill instructor asked. Several hands went up, and anticipating a ride in the jeep, recruits began listing their credentials. Everything from a degree in communications to a part-time job in a repair shop was declared. The DI listened to all the contenders, then pointed to the most qualified. "You," he barked. "Carry the radio."

— JIM SAPAUGH

As a flight instructor, one of my duties was to check out pilots who had been involved in aircraft accidents to ensure that they were proficient in emergency procedures. After completing one ride with a helicopter pilot whose engine had failed, the engine on my own helicopter suddenly gave out. As I initiated an emergency landing, I instructed my student to put out a mayday call on the radio. "Would you rather I take the controls?" he suggested. "After all, I've done this before."

— DANIEL M. JUNEAU

ONE UP

★ **The Right Stuff**

★ **Military "Maneuvers"**

While in the 101st Airborne Division at Fort Campbell, Ky., my husband would often pass the base mascot, an eagle in a large cage. The bird's name, Sergeant Glory, was even engraved on a nearby plaque. One morning my husband saw Sergeant Glory give his handler a nasty bite while being fed. The next day a new plaque appeared on the bird's enclosure. It read "Private Glory."

— ELISE DWOREK

At a tea for officers and their wives, the commanding general of a base delivered a seemingly endless oration. A young lieutenant grumbled to the woman sitting beside him, "What a pompous and unbearable old windbag that slob is!" The woman turned to him, her face red with rage. "Excuse me, Lieutenant. Do you have any idea who I am?" "No, ma'am," the man fumbled. "I am the wife of the man you just called an unbearable old windbag." "Oh," said the lieutenant. "And do you have any idea who I am?" "No," said the general's wife. "Thank God," said the lieutenant, getting up from his seat and disappearing into the crowd.

— MATT PARKER

My wife, Anita, worked at the Navy exchange dry cleaners while I was stationed at the submarine base in Groton, Conn. One evening a familiar-looking man in civilian clothes came to pick up his dry cleaning. Anita was sure he was on my crew and that she had met him at the "Welcome Aboard" family briefing a few weeks earlier. As she handed him his change, she said, "Excuse me, but aren't you on my husband's boat?" "No, ma'am," my commanding officer replied, "I believe your husband is on my boat."

— MICHAEL GORIUP

When my friend Brian was at a Marine Corps boot camp, a member of his unit was having little success on the firing range with his M-16 rifle—the poor guy couldn't hit targets at any distance. He was already frustrated when an angry drill instructor jumped in his face and berated him for poor marksmanship. "You can't hit a target at 50 yards!" the instructor bellowed. "Why, I'll bet you couldn't hit a target two inches in front of your face." "Of course I could," the recruit said. "But first you'll have to back up."

— J. L. SABIN

I knew my new golfing friend, Bill, had been in the Army, so after he arrived late for three tee times, I offered a good-natured jab at his tardiness. "Bill," I said, "I wonder what they used to say in the service when you were late for roll call?" "They always said the same thing whether I was late or not," he replied. " 'Good morning, Colonel.' "

— SOURCE UNKNOWN

While checking in for a short stay at Keesler Air Force Base in Biloxi, Miss., I overheard another visiting serviceman complaining about his accommodations. He had already had a confrontation with one person, a sergeant, but was not satisfied, so he moved over to a clerk and began to grill her for information. The clerk tried her best to remain calm, but the serviceman wouldn't let up. Finally, wishing to speak to a higher authority, he asked, "Who would the sergeant call if the building were on fire?" She eyed him coolly and said, "The fire department."

— BILLY CRESWELL

★ ★ ★ ★ ★ ★ ★ ★ ★ ★ ★

 **And these are for keeping my pants up.**

My son regaled me with stories about how they do things in the modern Air Force. Being an old Air Force man myself, I scoffed at their complicated methods. "That's not the way we did it when I was in the service," I said. "Yeah," he shot back. "But when you were in, there were only two pilots, Wilbur and Orville."

— TED SHIRLEY

The lieutenant wanted to use a pay phone but didn't have change for a dollar. He saw a private mopping the floors and asked him, "Soldier, do you have change for a dollar?" "I sure have, buddy," the private answered. Giving him a mean stare, the lieutenant said, "That's no way to address an officer. Let's try it again. Private, do you have change for a dollar?" "No, sir," the private replied.

— GEORGE MELLO

The Right Stuff

While on a Coast Guard cutter in Narragansett Bay, Rhode Island, my radar-room staff was being tested on navigating by radar. We were able to tell the bridge what course to steer, based on the land, buoys and other ships spotted on the screen. But we could never tell what type of ships they were—all we saw were blips. At one point, our radar operator identified a target as the Newport ferry, supplying its course and speed. After he received a top score, with extra credit for identifying the ship, I asked him how he had known what it was. He took the ferry schedule out of his pocket.

— DONALD J. KAYTON

Conducting a study of sexual behavior, a researcher poses this question to an older Air Force pilot: "When did you last make love?" "Nineteen fifty-nine," he answers. "That's an awfully long time," she says. "I suppose," says the pilot, glancing at his watch. "But it's only twenty-one fifteen now."

— JOHN CLEESE, in *Life and How to Survive It*

On one of our ROTC field-training exercises we were required to fire flares. A fellow cadet and I managed to misfire and start a brush fire. We immediately called range control, and they promptly responded with fire-fighting equipment to put out the blaze. I had to set off a second flare and it, too, misfired, causing another fire. Once again, I called range control. Two weeks later our unit received a commendation for quick fire reporting.

— CLAYTON AHLFIELD

Stopping for a light at a Florida intersection, I noticed the car in front of me was stalled. Another motorist had stopped to help the woman push her car out of the way, but they were getting nowhere. A white van pulled alongside the disabled vehicle. Out jumped six Marines in full dress uniform. They jogged in unison, three to each side of the car, and without breaking cadence rolled the vehicle around the corner and into a parking lot. They then saluted the driver and leapt back into their van, never missing a beat. The door closed, and the van rolled on.

— GAIL W. KEISLER

Docked in St. Thomas in the Caribbean, the first thing I noticed was graffiti that screamed, "Yankees, Go Home." Underneath, a sailor had scrawled,

"Red Sox, Free Drinks at the Bar."

— JASON CAIN

A new Navy wife, my sister, Gina, drove to Millington, Tenn., to join her husband. After an exhausting 18-hour drive, she pulled up to the gate and told the guard that her husband was stationed there. "Do you have a sticker?" the guard asked. "Ummm, yes, I do," she said, confused. "It's on the back." The sentry was skeptical as he walked to the rear of her car. But when he bent down to have a look, he smiled and waved her on. The sticker read "Go Navy."

— JAN ROLLYSON

Military "Maneuvers"

Everyone in my Army Reserve unit is required to complete an annual physical-fitness test. As my group neared the halfway point of our 2½-mile run last year, one of the monitors shouted, "It helps to focus on a point far out ahead of you!" "Yeah," agreed one of the veterans, "like my retirement."

— SFC. DAVID GRANT

I run sophisticated weather programs on multimillion-dollar supercomputers at a Navy center for environmental predictions. On the morning Hurricane Opal was heading for the Florida coast, my boss, a Navy commander, gave me detailed reports on the hurricane's status to pass along to a friend who has family in the area. Fascinated by his ability to summon up-to-date reports so quickly, I asked him how to do it. He gave me a puzzled look and said, "Simple. Go turn on the television and watch the Weather Channel."

— JOANNE MILLER

While I was attending an advanced infantry training class, the MPs decided to stage a drug raid in our barracks to break in the post's newest search dog. When I returned to my quarters later that evening, the sergeant informed me of the search. Alarmed at the tone of her voice, I became increasingly nervous as she described how the dog, straining at the leash, led the MPs to the bottom drawer of my dresser. A variety of scenarios raced through my mind, but none explained why the dog would behave that way. Finally the sergeant put me out of my misery. "Why," she asked, "did you have a ham sandwich in your dresser?"

— CAROL A. COOPER

Our new elementary school was raising the American flag for the first time. To make the day special, we invited a Marine Corps color guard to come out and perform the duty for us. The day before the ceremony, the Marine in charge of the unit called to confirm directions to the school. After doing so, he was asked by our secretary whether he was sending Marines who like children. There was a brief pause on the other end of the line before the man replied, "Ma'am, if I tell them to like children, they will like children."

— ANN CUNNINGHAM

I was a young, hard-charging Marine corporal stationed in Okinawa when I took a course in map reading. After completing it, I reported my success to the company office. The commanding officer, a crusty Vietnam veteran, congratulated me. Knowing the major was strict about haircuts, though, I braced myself for a reprimand because I had missed my weekly trim. Instead, he asked if I could help

him out using my new map-reading skills. Saying it would be a career-enhancing opportunity, he gave me precise coordinates and told me to report back to him with what I found. Eagerly I pulled out the map and a compass and followed it while daydreaming about a promotion to sergeant. And then I arrived at my destination—a barbershop.

— CHARLES B. BROWN, JR.

One night at Coast Guard boot camp, a talented shipmate entertained our barracks with uncanny impressions of various officers. While most of us were in stitches, our recruit company commander warned the comic to stop his antics. When he was ignored, the overzealous recruit snitched. The following morning, our resident comedian was summoned to the commander's office, where he was confronted by the three subjects of his impressions and ordered to imitate them to their faces. They found his performance hilarious and sent him on his way with one proviso: he tell the "bootlicker" to report to the commander's office immediately. That afternoon we had a new recruit company commander when our aspiring comedian was promoted to the "recently vacated position."

— MICHAEL C. CORSEN

I was loading our aircraft carrier with supplies when an ensign saw one of my friends spit on the hangar floor, which was already covered with oil and refuse. The officer was appalled. "Sailor," he demanded, "would you spit on your floor at home?" "No, sir," my friend replied. "But I wouldn't land airplanes on my roof either."

— MICKEY HOMAN

    Soon after graduating from the Primary Leadership Development Course at Fort Campbell in Kentucky, I bragged to my first sergeant about how well I did in the land-navigation exercise. Looking at me skeptically, the first sergeant handed me a map of the base, a compass and a set of coordinates. Then he ordered me to find his designated point and call in. When I reached the coordinates, it turned out to be the PX. I found a pay phone and contacted the first sergeant. "Great job!" he declared. "Now that you're there, could you bring me some lunch?"

— SGT. KENNETH J. ALMODOVAR

    When I was in Bosnia, a group of Marines returned from a four-day patrol in five beat-up Chevy pickups and ten Humvees. After receiving a box meal and a cup of coffee, the men wanted to shower at camp five miles away. A group headed for camp in the pickups. I was surprised to see the others wait in the rain for the pickups to return rather than drive the Humvees. I asked a gunnery sergeant why no one wanted to ride in the Humvees. Swallowing a gulp of coffee, he replied, "Humvees don't have cup holders."

— LT. G.A. KILLINGBECK

    While my wife and I were vacationing in Hawaii, we went to see the USS *Arizona* Memorial but got lost and ended up at a gate manned by a young Marine. After he gave me directions to the memorial, I thanked him and said, "Have a nice day." As I was about to leave he said, "Sir, I'm 20 years old, single and stationed in Hawaii. Every day is a nice day."

— MICHAEL CRAIN

Excellence First was the motto of my Army company at Fort Gordon, Ga., and we were required to repeat it every time we greeted an officer. One afternoon, however, I met a second lieutenant at the entrance of the building where I work and forgot to recite the motto. After receiving a scolding for my breach of protocol, I reached out to open the door for him, but he said, "No, allow me." As I walked through the open door, I nodded to him and said without thinking, "Excellence First!"

— JEFFREY A. HURSEY

As an Army media analyst for a military press information center in Sarajevo, one of our more monotonous tasks was editing the transcripts of our daily briefings and press conferences. During one conference, however, it was driven home to me how important this job was. After a British general had referred to snipers in the area as the "lunatic fringe" during a press conference, one of our young officers was reading the transcript when he piped up, "Sir, the transcribers apparently know who the snipers are!" "Who?" I asked with great interest. "The lunatic French!"

— CHESTER A. KROKOSKI, JR.

Going over our weekly training schedule one morning at our small Army garrison, we noticed that our annual trip to the rifle range had been canceled for the second time, but that our semiannual physical-fitness test was still on as planned. "Does it bother anyone else," one soldier asked, "that the Army doesn't seem concerned with how well we can shoot, yet is extremely interested in how fast we can run?"

— THOMAS L. HAMMOND

★ ★ ★ ★ ★ ★ ★ ★ ★ ★ ★

In officer's training at the Army's Aberdeen, Md., Proving Ground, our class received instruction on sophisticated equipment. During one class, I was fascinated by an expensive-looking computer. The instructor bragged that it was able to withstand nuclear and chemical attacks. I was duly impressed. But then the instructor abruptly stopped his lecture and turned to me. "Lieutenant, there will be no eating or drinking in my class," he snapped. "You'll have to get rid of that coffee!" "Sure… but why?" I inquired meekly. "Because," he scolded, "a coffee spill could ruin the keyboard."

— JEANNE T. WHITAKER

MILITARY WISDOM

★ **Just a Little Red Tape**

★ **Reading the Signals**

★ ★ ★ ★ ★ ★ ★ ★ ★ ★ ★

The military leaves nothing to chance, as shown by a Department of Defense manual that includes the definition of what a first page is: "If the document has no front cover, the first page will be the front page. If it has a cover, the first page is defined as the first page you see when you open the cover. In some documents, the title page and the first page may be the same."

— ELEUTERIO EVANGELISTA

Soldiers' combat clothing is not supposed to be ironed, according to an unwritten rule. That, however, did not prevent one sergeant from slightly massaging the regulation. "Gentlemen," said the sergeant to his troops, "I cannot order you to press your combat dress. Nevertheless, for tomorrow's parade, uniforms will be allowed only four wrinkles, with one wrinkle running directly down the center and rear of each leg."

— CAPT. JAMES FISHER

With several years of Army National Guard duty under his belt, my roommate applied for officer training. But his lifelong dreams were dashed after he failed the eye exam. "That's too bad," I sympathized. "Does that mean you now have to quit the Guard entirely?" "No, I get to keep my old job," he said. "Driving trucks."

— DIANE HASTINGS

Our bulletin announced the upcoming Secretary of the Army Awards, given to those who "reduce consumption of printed material. Submit nominations using DA Form 1256 (include six copies) plus all documentation."

— WILLIAM PAQUIN

I've concluded that the military has more rules than bullets. What convinced me? A simple memo. "To whom it may concern," it began innocently enough. "This memo was misdirected to my department and I am forwarding it on to you. I have erased my initials and initialed my erasure."

— BRUCE CARNAHAN

When his jeep got stuck in the mud during a war game, our commanding officer pointed to some men lounging around and told them to help. "Sorry, sir," said one. "We've been classified dead." "Okay," said the CO. Turning to his driver, he ordered, "Throw those dead bodies under the wheels to give us traction."

— CATHERINE MOUNT

It took forever, but dog tags for my new chief petty officer arrived just days before we were shipping out. Trouble was, the tags listed him as Catholic, not Protestant. "I really should get them replaced," he said. "Don't bother," I told him. "It'll be faster and easier to convert."

— LESTER E. STILLWELL

My father, a Navy man, had the good fortune to be stationed in Hawaii—but the bad fortune to have fair skin. One day, after spending many hours under the hot sun, he reported back to duty with a terrible sunburn. Expecting sympathy, he was, instead, reprimanded by his superiors and then written up for **"destruction of government property."**

— LORA TEBBETTS

★ ★ ★ ★ ★ ★ ★ ★ ★ ★

I was charged by the Coast Guard to buy a house near Station Rockland in Maine to be converted into military housing. But after many delays on our part, the owners' lawyer got antsy. "I don't like working with the government," the man said. "I'm not sure I'd even trust one of your checks." "I wouldn't worry," I replied. "Not only do we print our own checks, we also print the money to back them up."

— BRUCE HERMAN

While trying to order an Air Force publication online, I stumbled upon a unique way the staff had found to deal with their back-order troubles. They had resolved the

problems processing back orders, they said. "However, in order to implement the solution, we will have to cancel all back orders before we resume operations."

— JAMES WITMER

Just a Little Red Tape

My friend's husband, responsible for the overall closing of a military base, was reviewing voluminous files. He found some old records that were of no possible value, and sent a letter to Washington requesting permission to destroy them. The reply he received read as follows: "Permission is given to destroy the records, but please make triplicate copies of them first."

— JEANIE L. SORENSEN

"Working on nuclear submarines is not hazardous," a military lecturer insisted. The soldiers in the audience were skeptical, but he persisted. "For example," he said, "some seamen stay on board for three to four years. And at the same time, their wives give birth to perfectly healthy babies."

— DONCHO KAROVV

My son, Barry, came home from a three-month deployment aboard his submarine, and told us that one of the ways the sailors kept up morale was to make wooden cars out of kits and run derby races. "What do you do for a ramp?" my husband inquired. "Don't need one," Barry said. "We just put the cars on the floor and then tilt the sub."

— MARY C. RYAN

★ ★ ★ ★ ★ ★ ★ ★ ★ ★

I was scrubbing the bulkhead on the USS *Kitty Hawk* one Sunday when the loudspeaker announced: "Religious services. Maintain silence about the decks. Knock off all unnecessary work." An hour later, the opinion many of us held regarding our daily routine was confirmed with the announcement: "Resume all unnecessary work."

— KENNETH BOOKS

Reading the Signals

The military is known for two things: secrets and acronyms. When my husband's public-affairs unit was reorganized, these office names were proposed—News Operations, News Operations Technology, and News Operation Web. Or, in military acronym-speak, "NO, NOT, NOW."

— MONICA YACENDA

One of my jobs in the Army is to give service members and their families tours of the demilitarized zone in South Korea. Before taking people to a lookout point to view North Korea, we warn visitors to watch their heads climbing the stairs, as there is a low overhang. The tour guide, first to the top, gets to see how many people have not heeded his advice. On one tour I watched almost an entire unit hit their heads one after another as they came up the stairs. Curious, I asked their commander what unit they were from. "Military intelligence," he replied.

— EDWARD RAMIREZ

★ ★ ★ ★ ★ ★ ★ ★ ★ ★ ★

As I drove past the Post Exchange one afternoon, the pickup truck in front of me suddenly stopped. The driver shouted to a private on the sidewalk, "How do I get to the gym?" The PFC pointed ahead and instructed the driver to make several turns. The man in the truck didn't understand, so the PFC repeated his directions. Still confused, the truck driver shook his head. Finally I decided to help. I leaned out my window and yelled, "Left, right, left!" A wide grin appeared on the driver's face. "Thanks, Sarge," he called. "Now I've got it!"

— SFC BILL ROCHE

Before we could go on leave, my division had to endure a safety briefing from the base commander. As you can imagine, the Army is very thorough, and she left nothing to chance. "If you find that you are going to be delayed," said the commander, "you need to call 555-1234. If you are arrested, call 555-1235. And finally, call 555-1236 if you are a fatality."

— SGT. SHAWN BOIKO

A maxim of war is to confuse the enemy. This job description from the Army Handbook for Joint Actions proves that our military is on the leading edge of confusion. OPSDEP: Short for Operations Deputy. By JCS charter, the Army representative is the DCSOPS. However, the ADSOPS (JA), who is the DEPOPSDEP, may act for the OPSDEP on all joint matters. The use of the term OPSDEP also includes DEPOPSDEP. OPSDEPs, or DEPOPSDEPs, can approve papers for the JCS.

— ROSS AND KATHRYN PETRAS, *The Lexicon of Stupidity*

★ ★ ★ ★ ★ ★ ★ ★ ★ ★

Living near the Army's Yakima Training Center in Washington, I often see tanks and other military vehicles perform maneuvers in the nearby hills. One day I noticed a whole crowd of tanks and jeeps, along with tents and personnel, camped in a valley just off the freeway. The vehicles and tents were painted with camouflage colors, and also covered with nets and brush in order to conceal them from view. The scene would never have caught my eye—if it weren't for the brightly colored outhouses scattered across the entire camp.

— BEN HODGE

During my first night flight, I asked my instructor what to do if the engine failed. "Get the plane gliding in a controlled descent, attempt to restart the engine and make a Mayday call," he explained. "The difference between day and night flying is that the terrain below will not be clearly visible, so turn on the landing light when you get close to the ground, and if you like what you see, land." "All right, but what if I don't like what I see?" I asked. "Turn off the landing light."

— SOURCE UNKNOWN

During his re-enlistment interview, the first sergeant asked my friend if he'd considered re-upping in the Air Force. "I wouldn't re-enlist if you made me a four-star general, gave me a million dollars and Miss America for a roommate!" he seethed. On the form, the first sergeant wrote, "Airman is undecided."

— BILL BACHMAN

★ ★ ★ ★ ★ ★ ★ ★ ★ ★ ★

Tax day—April 15—was looming when an elderly woman showed up at my desk at the IRS. She said she required a thick stack of tax forms. "Why so many?" I asked. "My son is stationed overseas," she said. "He asked me to pick up forms for the soldiers on the base." "You shouldn't have to do this," I told her. "It's the base commander's job to make sure that his troops have access to the forms they need." "I know," said the woman. "I'm the base commander's mother."

— DONNA BELL

In Army basic training, we were required to crawl facedown on the ground under barbed-wire fencing with machine guns firing blank ammunition above us. Since I am six feet, six inches tall, however, it was impossible for me to accomplish this without my rear end sticking up in the air. No matter how hard I tried or how loudly the sergeant yelled, I couldn't keep my behind down. "Well, Private Olson," the sergeant said after I finally completed one obstacle course, "one thing's for sure—you'll never take a bullet in the head!"

— ANDRA M. OLSON

During inspection, I was hoping—praying—that our gnarly-looking sergeant would find nothing wrong with my sleeping area. He did. But much to my surprise, he was quite philosophical about it. "Son, when you're born you come from dust, and when you die you return to dust," he intoned. "Now, someone is either coming or going underneath your bed and you better get him cleaned up."

— WILLIAM GERBER

"Who here speaks French?" demanded our sergeant. Three guys raised their hands. "Good," he said. "You get to clean the latrine. That's a French word."

— JAMES CONAHAN

A senior in high school, and a few years away from becoming a U.S. citizen, I received a recruiting call from the Army. After listening intently to how I would have my college tuition paid for, not to mention the many benefits of serving my country, I told the officer that while I was very interested, there was one problem: I was Libyan. "That's okay," he answered understandingly. "We take liberals too."

— KOLOUD TARAPOLSI

Go FIGuRE

★ **Think Again**

★ **Don't Ask**

★ **Getting By**

I was standing on the shore of a lake in Fort Polk, La., showing some soldiers how to use a compass, when I heard a collective gasp from the group. I quickly wheeled around only to catch sight of a huge alligator crouching in the mud no more than five feet away. Before I could flee for my life, one of my guys let me know I should take my time. "Don't worry, Sarge, he ain't movin'," he shouted. "He fell asleep listening to you too."

— LARRY THOMPSON

Because of the constant movement in the military, our headquarters command marked parking spaces with acronyms representing the various job titles worthy of reserved spots. A new staff sergeant was immediately struck by the variety of vehicles owned by the person assigned one particularly choice slot—it seemed a different model was parked there each day. Curious, he looked through the base phone book to find out who was in charge of "FCFS," as the space was marked. Finally, unable to come up with the answer, he asked his coworkers if they knew. That's when he learned the acronym stood for "**F**irst **C**ome, **F**irst **S**erved."

— CAPT. JAMEY CIHAK

Sitting in basic communications training, we were having trouble understanding some concepts of satellite technology. "Come on, guys," the instructor said, "this isn't rocket science." After an uncomfortable pause, a courageous trainee raised his hand and said, "Sir, I'm no genius, but since we are dealing with launching satellites, I believe this actually is rocket science."

— JON REINSCH

As a professor at Southwest Baptist University in Bolivar, Mo., I often begin class by telling a story about my son who attends the U.S. Naval Academy. Last December, one ingenious student left me a note on the blackboard, wishing me a merry Christmas with the following words: "Feliz Navydad!"

— BING B. BAYER

There were tons of vending machines on base, and as the supply sergeant, I was responsible for all of them. So I pulled in a private and had him count the money. An hour later, he was finished. "Good," I said. "What's the count?" He replied, "I have 210 quarters, 180 dimes and 35 nickels."

— DAVID MORRIS

A friend was visiting me at Davis-Montham Air Force Base and asked me to explain various acronyms. I told him PCS means permanent change of station, NCOIC stands for noncommissioned officer in charge, and TDY is used for temporary duty. Later, we were visiting the ruins of an old fort. I mentioned that an assignment there must have been very tedious. My friend asked, "What's TDS?"

— ROBERT WIDO

Think Again

One day a young Air Force enlisted man walked into the base newspaper office where I work and said he'd like to place an advertisement. "Classified?" I asked. "No, ma'am," he replied with great seriousness. "It's unclassified."

— MONICA COSTELLO

 Talk about service.

While attending a formal military dinner with my boyfriend, an Army National Guardsman, I was baffled by the number of acronyms that were used. Finally I turned to the colonel next to me and said, "You should have a translator here for civilians. I don't speak 'Acronym.'" "I guess I never thought about it," he said apologetically. "So what do you do for a living?" "Oh," I replied, "I work for a CPA."

— URSULA KLEIN

My squad leader decided to try to break the base record of 424 push-ups. With our physical-training instructor standing over him, he knocked out 100 quick ones before he settled into a steady rhythm. We were sure he'd break the record, but at 390 he paused at the top and began to shake his head from side to side before slowly continuing. After finishing his 402nd push-up, he paused again, shook his head, coughed, then collapsed. As we walked back to our barracks, our instructor cracked a rare smile. "You gotta give that guy credit," he said. "If he had just been able to shake that wasp away from his face instead of inhaling it, he'd have broken the record for sure."

— MSGT. PATRICK L. HATHAWAY

Two days before officers-training graduation, I bragged that my single demerit was the lowest in the company. The next day I saw with chagrin a slip on my bunk, and was thoroughly humbled when I read the list: 1 Demerit: Littering. Penny under bed. 1 Demerit: Lincoln needs a shave and a haircut. 1 Demerit: Trying to bribe an officer. 1 Demerit: Bribe not enough.

— FREDERIC P. SEITZ

My daughter recently returned from Iraq on a civilian airplane. Before boarding, she and her squad went through the metal detectors. She'd forgotten she had her Swiss army knife in her pocket, and it was confiscated. Upset, she joined the other soldiers as they boarded the plane, carrying their M-16 rifles.

— MICHAEL DELUCA

    Crew cut, flattop, buzz cut…. Whatever you call them, military haircuts are not always the height of fashion. And even the military recognizes that. While passing a U.S. armed services barbershop in Heidelberg, Germany, I saw these rates that were posted in the window: Haircuts: $7 Military Haircuts: $6

— ERIC GERENCSER

    At the Oceana, Va., Naval Air Station, I was training a young ground-crew member on how to direct an F-14 into the fuel pit. I glanced over to check wing clearance and, when I looked back, discovered that he had taxied the aircraft too far forward for the fuel hose to reach. "You'll have to send him around again," I informed the trainee. "What?" he said, surprised. "They spend millions on these things and you can't put them in reverse?"

— JOHN G. RUTGERS

    Flashlights used by my National Guard unit can withstand almost anything. And to prove it, they come with a lifetime warranty. Nevertheless, nothing is indestructible, which is why the warranty also cautions, "Void with shark bites, bear attacks and children under the age of five."

— CARMEN HILL

    As a Marine captain stationed in Okinawa, Japan, I was accompanying the assistant commandant on his inspection of the troops. To break the silence, the general would ask some of the Marines standing at attention which outfit they were serving with. Ramrod straight, each would respond, "Marine Air Group 36, sir," or "Second Marine Division,

General." But near the end of the inspection, when the general asked a young private, "Which outfit are you in?" the Marine replied, "Dress blues, sir, with medals!"

— JOHN D. BRATTEN

Although fighting the enemy is considered normal, the Army frowns upon fighting among the troops. So much so that after one too many battles royal, my uncle was ordered to undergo a psychiatric evaluation in which he had to endure some odd questions. "If you saw a submarine in the Sahara, what would you do?" "Well, I'd throw snowballs at it," he answered. "Where'd you get the snowballs?" the doctor asked. "Same place you got the submarine."

— HANNAH ETCHISON

I was playing cards on my bunk by myself when I suddenly felt a presence looming over my shoulder. It was a young private. "Excuse me," the private finally said, as he tried to follow the game. "What are you playing?" "Solitaire," I replied. "Oh," he said, as he walked away. "I didn't know you could play that without a computer."

— ROBERT OWENS

Safety is job one in the Air Force. Overstating the obvious is job two, as I discovered when crawling into my military-issue sleeping bag. The label read:

"In case of an emergency, unzip and exit through the top."

— KEITH J. WALTERS

While my brother-in-law was in the Army, he had a desk job and his own office. At coffee breaks, he listened to officers complain about how they couldn't get their work done with all the interruptions. Once he got promoted, he knew what they were talking about. That's when they changed the nameplate on his door—to Corporal Meeting, from Private Meeting.

— JEANNE HAYNES

Don't Ask

Stationed on Guam, I was part of the SEAL team conducting a training mission to simulate terrorist activity. In the early hours of the morning, our duty officer called the area commander to report that the SEALs had cut a hole in the base perimeter fencing, broken into a building and taken hostages. Sleepily, the commander asked our duty officer if the hole in the fence was simulated. "Yes, sir" was his reply. "And were the break-in and hostages simulated?" After another affirmative answer, the commander asked, "Then why didn't you simulate this phone call?"

— RICHARD DESMOND

While on my desk assignment in the Army, I noticed that my coworker Rick never answered his phone. One day I asked him why. "If you had to pick up the telephone and say, 'Statistical section, Specialist Strasewski speaking,'" Rick replied indignantly, "you wouldn't want to answer it either!"

— KATHERINE FIDDLER

I arrived in Texas on a warm fall day, ready to begin my tour as an exchange student from the Canadian armed forces. When I met the commanding officer, he pointed out how lucky I was to be in his state at this time of year. "Yes, sir," I agreed, "the weather here is much better than back in Ontario." "Weather?" said the colonel. "I'm talking about football season!"

— MICHAEL KYTE

One night my husband, Lee, a retired Army colonel, was watching a program on TV about paratroopers. As one D-Day jumper began to comment, my husband exclaimed, "That's Jack Norton! I served in both Korea and Vietnam with him." Then, after watching the man speak for a few moments, Lee quietly remarked, "You know you're getting old when you have more friends on the History Channel than in the news."

— SHERRY H. FAIR

The executive officer of the unit where I worked in the National Guard Armory went to a government office to take care of some business. The clerk there gave him two index cards with identical questions on them. The officer filled both out, but when he handed them in, he asked the clerk why she needed two cards with the same information. Stapling the cards together, she said, "That's in case we lose one."

— BILL JOHNSON

When my husband was a civilian working overseas for the Air Force, he entered a golf tournament sponsored by the air base in Moron, Spain. He won the tournament, but he has always been reluctant to show off his award. The trophy reads, "First Prize Moron."

— FONTAINE CHASE

When my son joined the Marine Corps, his cousin was already an Army officer. The two were home on leave at the same time, and had a wonderful time exchanging stories. But after hearing one Marine joke too many, my son finally chastised his cousin with: "Man, haven't you learned what ARMY stands for?" "No, what?" "Ain't Ready for Marines Yet."

— ANNE HICKS

At the maritime museum where I work, we occasionally use midshipmen to do the "dirty work" of restoring a 100-year-old cruiser. One day the Navy sent a crew of 20 men, while the Marines sent a crew of three. Teasing one Navy midshipman, I said, "You mean it takes twenty Navy guys to do the work of only three Marines?" "Sir, no, sir," he snapped back. "The truth is, sir, it takes six or seven of us to supervise each one of those Marines!"

— BRIAN SMITH

Glenn, my husband, is stationed in Belgium, where his job includes proofreading English documents written by European officers. Once a German lieutenant colonel brought him a lengthy paper. "I should have my wife look it over," Glenn said. "She's an English major." "Oh," the colonel replied, "I didn't realize your wife was in the British army."

— ANNA MAGGARD

★ ★ ★ ★ ★ ★ ★ ★ ★ ★

Getting By

While reading our headquarters' monthly training report, I noticed that it included a motto, "Committment to Excellence." I immediately notified the office that produces the report that commitment had but one "t" in the middle. On our next report, our motto had changed to "Committed to Excellence."

— WERNER WOLF

During an exercise, I heard a radio transmission between a captain and a lieutenant who was a new platoon leader. After the lieutenant reported over an unsecured radio network that the unit was located at a certain map coordinate, the captain told his young charge that he should not give his location "in the clear." The lieutenant replied, "We're not in the clear. The platoon is located in the woods next to the farmer's barn."

— MAJ. RON MCCANDLESS

A friend recently went through Army Ranger training in Florida. During the second day of the brutal "swamp phase," as the soldiers were rowing an inflatable raft down a river, a fishing boat cruised by with two scantily clad sunbathers on deck. The harsh rigors of the training suddenly came into focus when my friend turned to his buddy and asked, "I wonder if they had any food in that cooler?"

— SAVOY WILSON

When my family lived on Okinawa, one of the biggest events of the year was the military's Fourth of July celebration, which culminated in a spectacular fireworks display. One year, as we joined the early evening crowd on the improvised midway, we watched with alarm as three tipsy airmen headed for the commanding officer. One of the men ambled up to the general and, without even a salute, cheerfully swatted his arm. "Say," the airman inquired, "what time do the fireworks start?" The general eyed him coolly for a moment then replied, "Any minute, son. Any minute."

— MEG FAVILLE

A friend often told me about the problems he had getting his son to clean his room. The son would always agree to tidy up, but then wouldn't follow through. After high school the young man joined the Marine Corps. When he came home for leave after basic training, his father asked him what he had learned in the service. "Dad," he said. "I learned what 'now' means."

— JAN KING

My son-in-law had just joined the Navy and had gone for a walk downtown to show off his brand-new uniform. After passing a few restaurants and bars, he decided to stop off for a refreshment. A waitress came over to him and said, "Draft, sir?" "Nope," he replied. **"Enlisted."**

— BARBARA COOK

A quality-control clerk, I once was stationed at a Florida Navy base with a chief petty officer who had an attaché case identical to mine. The cases were stylish and durable, but it was nearly impossible to tell which side was the top. One day, after the chief spilled pens and papers on the floor of our office, he got fed up. He grabbed a can of spray paint and wrote "TOP" on the case. But he hadn't turned the case over before marking it, and I did all I could not to laugh at his mistake. "I can't believe I did that," he finally said with disgust. "I know," I said, chuckling. "You painted the bottom of your case." "It's worse than that," he said. "This isn't my case."

— BRUCE FRAZIER

My husband, a Marine Corps drill instructor, walked into the barracks after boot-camp graduation and saw a new Marine and his family circling one of the large metal trash cans. When my husband asked his former charge what he was doing, the man replied, "Just showing my family the alarm clock."

— LISA M. JONES

At Travis Air Force Base in California, I was assigned to the electronic-component repair section of my shop. Because of the electrical hazards of the job, we were forbidden to wear watches and rings while performing our duties. One day our foreman walked through our area and admonished one of my coworkers for wearing a watch while repairing a part. "Oh, it's okay," the worker protested. "This watch says it's 'shock-resistant.'"

— SOURCE UNKNOWN

Thinking FAST

★ **So They Say**

★ **You Can't Win 'em All**

While stationed in Washington, D.C., I used Arlington National Cemetery as a shortcut on my way to give a briefing at Fort Myer. To my surprise, I encountered a roadblock manned by the military police. An MP approached my car and asked in a stern voice, "Are you supposed to be here?" Unsure of what to say, I replied, "Not yet." He held back a smile and waved me on.

— DAVID T. LIPP

When I was stationed in Germany with the Air Force, we worked side by side with the Army but were governed by different regulations. One rule involved what we were allowed to do while on various watches. Those of us in the Air Force were allowed to read anything we wished, while Army members could read only manuals or, in some cases, nothing at all. One night during a long watch, one of my friends was quietly reading a comic book when an Army captain stormed over. "You know, the Army can't read here!" she said sternly. "That's okay," the airman replied calmly. "When I'm finished I'll let them look at the pictures."

— RHONDA ROLZ

During last summer's drought in Oklahoma, National Guard units were mobilized to assist by hauling in hay from other states. On one trip, I passed a convoy of National Guard trucks, each carrying 14 large hay bales. Chalked on the bumper of the lead truck was

"Operation Cow Chow."

— VIRGINIA BARLOW

Shortly after graduating from high school, my brother, Roger, joined the Air Force. We missed him terribly, and to make matters worse, he wasn't allowed to use the phone. After about two weeks my family was awakened in the middle of the night by the ringing telephone. Fearing something had happened to Roger, I hurriedly picked up the receiver and was relieved to hear his voice. "What happened?" I said. "I thought no one was allowed to call out?" "We're not," he answered. "But they left me guarding the phone!"

— KIMBER E. BUSH

During a recent joint exercise a Navy admiral repeatedly called a veteran Marine master sergeant "chief," the Navy's equivalent rank. On the last day of the operation, the admiral caught himself again calling the Marine "chief" and said, "I'm sorry, master sergeant, but if you were in the Navy, you would be a chief." "No, sir," the Marine replied. "If I were in the Navy, I'd be an admiral."

— CHRIS LAWSON

One of my first assignments as an Army lieutenant was to report to the contract-management detachment of the Boeing Company, maker of the Minuteman nuclear missile. As I rode the elevator to meet my commander, it stopped, and a Boeing employee entered. "Four, please," he said. I mistakenly pushed the button for the third floor. As I realized my error, the man from Boeing commented, "We're very happy to have you here, Lieutenant… and not in a missile silo."

— BRYAN PIERNOT

THINKING FAST ★

★ ★ ★ ★ ★ ★ ★ ★ ★ ★ ★

As recruits at Lackland Air Force Base in San Antonio, we had a duty called "dorm guard." A rookie was required to stand a one-hour shift at the door of his dorm, allowing only authorized personnel to enter, and alerting the unit to the presence of an officer by calling everyone to attention. A colonel had been in the dorm for several minutes when we heard the guard call, "Atten-hut!" Everyone snapped to rigid attention awaiting the oncoming officer. In walked a lieutenant. Our drill instructor, realizing that the unwitting guard had called a colonel to attention for a subordinate officer, ran over to the guard and yelled, "You have a colonel standing at attention for a lieutenant! What are you going to do about this?" In his most commanding voice, the recruit shouted out, "Colonel, at ease!"

— KENNETH R. MCALISTER

When my son Jordan was graduating from Navy boot camp, parents were anxious to see their sons and daughters after what for most people had been the longest separation in their lives. When the ceremony began, the guest speaker noted that he'd had a conversation with a fellow officer regarding the topic to address. "What should I talk about?" he'd asked his colleague. "Considering the families haven't seen their recruits in nine weeks," the officer replied, "I'd say about two minutes."

— SUSAN RASH

> During a review of radar basics, I asked some Coast Guard sailors, "What's the difference between a 2D radar and a 3D radar?" The genius in the front row answered, **"1D."**
>
> — ROBERT KIPKE

Increasingly in the military, members of one branch are required to work with members of another, and sometimes this causes trouble. A friend, while working on a joint deployment, saw a veteran Army master sergeant become frustrated at a perceived lack of respect from a young Air Force airman. The master sergeant pointed to the six stripes arranged on his shoulder and asked his young counterpart, "Do you know what three up and three down mean?" "Sure," the young airman replied. "The end of an inning."

— RAY FARRELL

So They Say

One day I was all set to give a presentation at the Naval War College in Newport, R.I. When I learned that I was scheduled to be the final speaker, it was a point of pride for me. "In a relay race," I explained to a colleague, "the final runner is called the anchor. You always put your best runner in the anchor position." "But this is the Navy," my friend retorted. "In the Navy they throw the anchor overboard."

— TONY SCHULTZ

One coworker told me about a military funeral he attended. Everything went perfectly until one of the soldiers carrying the casket slipped and fell into the freshly dug grave. The crowd gasped and the officer in charge turned white. The young soldier, however, was a quick thinker. He pulled himself out and stated in a commanding voice, "Sir, the grave is fit for burial."

— FIRST LT. DAR PLACE

When my husband was a psychological operations company commander at Fort Bragg, a new first sergeant arrived who wanted the soldiers to clean up the area. At his initial formation, the sergeant bent down and picked up a piece of paper. "This is a signed four-day pass," he read, "to whoever brings this in to the first sergeant of A Company." Hoping to find another, the soldiers quickly picked up every scrap of paper, and the company area was the cleanest in the battalion.

— MELODY ALEGRE

With our aircraft carrier under way on an important exercise, the admiral called all of the pilots together to discuss safety. He sternly lectured the group, then glared at them and asked gruffly, "Any questions?" No one said a word, so he asked a second time. Still no takers. "No one is leaving," he demanded, "until I get a question." "So," came a weak voice from the back, "where you from?"

— JEFFRY L. EDGAR

The day before graduation from Army basic training, I stood on the edge of a blazing hot parade field watching a group of soldiers rake the freshly cut grass. Suddenly, a helicopter appeared and made a practice landing in anticipation of delivering a dignitary the following day. The sergeant in charge of the raking detail ran to the chopper and spoke to the pilot. He then jogged off the field, taking his group with him. The helicopter lifted off, made a few low passes over the field, then flew away. I asked the sergeant what maneuver the pilot had been practicing. He smiled and said, "Grass removal."

— ROBERT L. SELSER

The colonel who served as inspector general in our command paid particular attention to how personnel wore their uniforms. On one occasion he spotted a junior airman with a violation. "Airman," he bellowed, "what do you do when a shirt pocket is unbuttoned?" The startled airman replied, "Button it, sir!" The colonel looked him in the eye and said, "Well?" At that, the airman nervously reached over and buttoned the colonel's shirt pocket.

— G. DEARING, JR.

I was walking through the barracks of the Air Force unit I commanded in the Philippines when I noticed that a few of the airmen had posters of scantily clad young women on their lockers. I immediately told the sergeant in charge that only pictures of family members could be displayed. A few days later I went back through the barracks and saw that one of the posters remained, but that it now had an inscription. "To Joe," it read, "Love, Sis."

— ROBERT P. GATES

During survival training at Coast Guard boot camp, we were required to jump from a 30-foot-high platform into a swimming pool. One of my fellow recruits went to the edge of the platform but immediately backed off. The drill instructor quickly showed his disapproval. "What would you do if you had to abandon a burning, sinking ship?" he snapped. Eyeing the distance to the water, the recruit replied, "I'd wait until the ship sank a little lower before jumping."

— ZEKE CANDLER

★ ★ ★ ★ ★ ★ ★ ★ ★ ★ ★

You Can't Win 'em All

After completing a celestial navigation training course in the Navy, I was eager to show off my new knowledge of the stars to my date for the evening. "That's Regulus," I said confidently, "and there's Polaris, the North Star." Impressed, she pointed to a bright light on the horizon. "And what is that?" she asked. "Oh, that's Venus," I replied. "Note the steady light typical of planets." Her awe quickly turned to amusement, however, when "Venus" slowly drew nearer, turned and began to lower its wheels for landing.

— KERRY ANDERSON CROOKS

I was a young Reserve first lieutenant on an assignment with some seasoned Marines. When it was time to return to base for chow, we discovered our bus wouldn't start. Not wanting the men to be late for dinner, our sergeant major suggested taking them back in the dump truck. So the Marines piled into the truck while the sergeant major took the wheel and I settled in beside him. As we were driving along, I said, "We shouldn't leave that bus here unattended, should we?" "No," he replied, "but I'm not concerned. We have something else to be worried about." "What's that?" I asked. "We're not supposed to be hauling people in a dump truck," he said. "But we have a bigger worry than that." "What?" I asked, getting nervous. "I don't have a license to drive a dump truck," he said. "But you know, that doesn't worry me at all." "Why not?" I replied. "Because," he said with a smirk, "you're in charge."

— LYNDA REARICK

When my husband visited our son, Michael, at boot camp, he found him marching smartly with his unit. Michael's father proudly approached the soldiers and began to snap photo after photo. Embarrassed and worried about getting into trouble, Michael looked straight ahead and didn't change his expression. Suddenly his drill sergeant barked, "Comito, give me 25 push-ups. And the next time your daddy wants your picture, you smile!"

— EDYTHE COMITO

When I was transferred to an Army unit in Germany, I immediately tried to put my high-school German to use. It was going well until one night on the subway. Sitting across from a nicely dressed couple, I initiated a conversation in German and asked for directions to a local shopping district. All this took about a minute. When I finally stopped talking, the woman looked at her husband and in a Southern drawl said, "Keep smiling, honey, and he'll go away."

— JAMES S. HOUK II

My brother, Shawn, was working the graveyard shift on an Air Force security detail in Germany when he fell asleep against the wheel of his vehicle. He was awakened only when the guard shack announced over his radio that his relief had arrived. "Get a good night's sleep?" my brother was asked by his sergeant back at the shack. "Oh, no, sir, I was wide awake," Shawn replied. "What makes you think I was sleeping?" "Airman," the sergeant said. "Look in the mirror." My brother looked in the mirror and grinned sheepishly when he saw the unmistakable Mercedes-Benz logo imprinted on his forehead.

— ROBERT F. FALCONER II

When a friend of mine was an Air Force base commander, he sent one of his formal, or "mess dress," uniforms to a tailor for alterations. After a few days the seamstress, who had a heavy German accent, called his office to say the uniform was finished. The secretary wrote down the message and handed it to an enlisted man for delivery. The airman entered the commander's office but was hesitant to say why he was there. The colonel asked what the young man wanted. Frustrated by his stammering, he ordered, "Out with it!" The enlisted man looked at him sheepishly and said, "Your mistress is ready."

— WYNNE YOUNG

During an important military exercise, another Air Force member and I were working in a radar van under a simulated attack. We were under strict orders not to open the door unless we received the secret code, which we had been given at the morning briefing. Later in the day, we heard knocking at the door. Remembering our orders, I yelled out "Fort" and waited for the correct response, "Knox." It never came. Several minutes later we heard more knocking, but again we didn't receive the proper response. Over the course of the afternoon, various others came to the door and knocked, but no one gave us the correct password. Proud of ourselves for not being tricked into opening up to the enemy, we later received a phone call from a furious superior officer who told us to open the door immediately. After we explained that we were simply following orders, he informed us that the code was not "Fort Knox," but four knocks.

— LYNDA C. LOVELL

I was standing at attention with a number of other recruits outside an airport in San Diego, eagerly awaiting the bus that would take us to Marine Corps boot camp. But our enthusiasm began to wane, and a creeping feeling of apprehension took its place. So it was no surprise when I heard a young man behind me say, "I think I've made a mistake." Not wishing to break my military bearing, I stared straight ahead and softly said out of the side of my mouth, "I know what you mean, but I'm trying to remain optimistic. I figure it's only 12 weeks, and it will all be worth it when we graduate and become Marines." "Thanks for clearing that up," came the whispered reply. "I thought this was the line for my rental-car shuttle bus."

— DAMIAN ROSSITTIS

 **Are we there yet?**

Shortly after my cousin joined the Navy, my aunt repeatedly warned him about the dangers of getting a tattoo. To placate her, my cousin reluctantly agreed to call her should he ever contemplate getting one. The dreaded call finally came. My aunt thanked him for keeping his word, then surprisingly gave him her blessing without further questioning. My cousin was surprised at her attitude and pressed her for the reason she agreed so quickly. With a deep sigh of resignation, my aunt replied, "Because your younger sister came home with one the other day."

— B. FOLISI

Our six-week training camp at Fort Bragg, N.C., was capped by a traditional military graduation ceremony. With all of the families gathered in the stands, our commanding general watched the formation from his podium. After the Army Band played the national anthem, a three-cannon salute to the colors boomed across the parade grounds. The general was due to speak next, but his remarks were delayed—until the wailing of dozens of car alarms ended.

— DENNIS W. LAHMANN

As a professor at the Air Force Institute of Technology, I taught a series of popular courses on software engineering. The program was highly competitive and difficult to get into, but one prospective student made our decision whether to accept him quite simple. When asked to fax over his college transcript, the student told me, "Well, I would, but it's the only copy that I've got."

— JIM SKINNER

A friend had just completed Marine Corps recruit training at Parris Island, S.C., when his grandparents came to visit. Eager to show how proud they were of their young Marine, the couple went to a store where the grandfather bought a T-shirt emblazoned with the Marine Corps emblem. He immediately put it on before returning to the base, but soon noticed he was getting odd looks from passers-by. Later, when the man looked more closely at his new shirt, he realized why. Above the emblem was printed, "My boyfriend is a Marine."

— JOHN LICHTENWALNER

As a newly commissioned infantry lieutenant, I was eager to set an example for my platoon by cleaning my own M-16 rifle. While we were working on the weapons, one soldier complained about the unusual notched shape of the M-16's bolt and chamber, which makes it difficult to clean. "Lieutenant, they need to make something to clean this with," the soldier said. "They do," piped up a sergeant. "Really," I said with surprise, wondering why we had not ordered such a tool. "Yes, sir," replied the sergeant. "It's called a soldier."

— CHARLES ANDERSON

While in the Army, my son Gabe attended POSH (Prevention of Sexual Harassment) classes. During one session, the sergeant said to his men, "Before you tell a joke, ask yourselves, What would my mother think?" Gabe replied, "Sergeant, there's a problem with that." "What is it?" "If I listened to what my mother had to say, I wouldn't have joined the Army in the first place."

— ANGELA TRAYNOR

My nephew, Chris, was assigned to drive in a truck convoy one night while serving in the Marine Corps. When he pulled away, he noticed the truck behind him was following much too closely. When he sped up, so did the other truck. When he slowed down, so did the other truck. He became concerned that the other driver would cause an accident. When he turned a corner and pulled up to the guard station, he noticed that the driver behind him had cut the turn too sharply and knocked down part of the gate. "He's been tailgating me since we left," Chris explained to the guard. "And look, now he's knocked down part of the gate." The guard eyed him coolly and said, "Corporal, you are towing the truck behind you."

— MARIE N. GOFORTH

The young training instructor at Lackland Air Force Base, fresh out of TI school, was doing everything by the book. Our group of 50 female basic trainees was gathered around as he showed us how to fold and hang our clothes military style. Using one of the women's lockers as an example, he referred to his TI school guide, fumbling with T-shirts and socks as he attempted to fold them into the prescribed shapes. Taking another long glance at the book, he reached into the locker and pulled out a set of lacy women's underwear. After a few awkward moments, he gave up. "Okay," he said, "just fold them like your mother taught you."

— DENISE L. FOX

★ ★ ★ ★ ★ ★ ★ ★ ★ ★ ★

A sergeant in my Army bomb-clearing detail was asked to conduct a class for a group of visiting officers. Needing a prop to demonstrate, the sergeant retrieved a live bomb from the impact area. One class member, a second lieutenant, seemed nervous about a live bomb being used for the demo. He kept interrupting the class with, "Sergeant, I know you've done this before, but are you sure that you're doing it right?" After the fourth interruption, a voice called from the back of the room, "Lieutenant, I guarantee that in all your military career, you'll never meet anyone who's done this before and done it wrong!"

— DARRELL SMITH

While going through basic training in Texas, we were taught the Army's phonetic alphabet. Once when being quizzed by our drill sergeant, I had to give the representation for the letter "m." My mind went blank. I reasoned that since the letter "p" was represented by Papa, then "m" must be Mama. Looking forlornly at the sergeant, I bellowed, "Mama!" "Son," the sergeant responded, breaking into a grin, "even your mama can't help you now!"

— JOE LEE STOREY

At sea aboard the USS *Saipan*, I was passing by the ship's galley and overheard two sailors—a veteran and a new seaman—talking while they were on mess duty. "Hey, Bill," asked the younger, "what's the difference between a cook and a chef?" "Simple," answered his shipmate, "a chef doesn't have tattoos."

— K. I. SEPP

Tinker Air Force Base in Oklahoma was readying for an important inspection. Part of the sidewalk in front of the base commander's building was damaged, so a new section of concrete was poured to replace it. However, the new concrete did not match the darker color of the old sidewalk. Several remedies were suggested, but none could be completed in time for the inspection. "All right, men," an exasperated captain said, "let's smear some mud over the new section to match the colors." "Congratulations, sir," said the chief master sergeant. "Now you're thinking like an enlisted man!"

— STEVEN A. HOSELTON

When I came back to the United States after a tour of duty with the Marines in Vietnam, I stayed with my parents for a 30-day leave. Mom's rules were simple: I could come and go as I pleased, but I had to let her know when I returned home each night. After one long evening with friends, I crept into the house and didn't knock on Mom's door. Late the next morning when I came down for breakfast, she glared at me with icy silence. "Look, Mom," I said, "I'm sorry I didn't tell you I got home safely last night, but what did you do all the time I was in Vietnam?" "Well," she replied, "at least then I knew where you were!"

— BILL BRUCKNER

HuH?

★ **Another Language?**

★ **Come Again?**

★ **Some Reassurance**

★ ★ ★ ★ ★ ★ ★ ★ ★ ★ ★

When you're stationed in Germany, you tend to have different priorities. A sign on our squadron's microwave read: "Do not use when coffeemaker is on. The circuit breaker will blow up and catch the beer on fire."

— DON HAMILTON

Stationed overseas with the Air Force, my wife and I collected miniature statues. Two of our favorites were replicas of the "Winged Victory" and "Venus de Milo." When we returned to the States and unpacked our boxes, our attention was drawn to the container holding our collection. The military movers, in an effort to protect themselves from liability, had written on the outside of the box: "Small statues; two already damaged—one missing head, another missing arms."

— LT. COL. LAYNE E. FLAKE

Before I could visit my daughter at her naval base in Japan, I was told I needed to supply her with some important information to give to security. The list included the following: passport number, height, weight, year of birth and anticipated hair color at time of arrival.

— DIXIE MCFARLAND

I drove my daughter to a weekend boot camp for teenagers sponsored by the Army. When we arrived, we didn't know whom to talk to. We asked a guy at the front desk, who nodded vaguely toward one of the officers standing behind him. Seeing my confusion, he added, "You can't miss him—he's wearing camouflage."

— K. L. CAMPBELL

★ ★ ★ ★ ★ ★ ★ ★ ★ ★

My husband, daughter and son-in-law are active in the Civil Air Patrol, the auxiliary of the Air Force. Recently they all attended a state conference, where my daughter told me her father would be receiving an award. The evening of the banquet, my husband called home, and I asked how it was going. "Oh, pretty good," he said, and we chatted about it. I wondered why he didn't say anything about the award, but, fearing that he hadn't gotten it after all, I didn't mention it. When he returned home, he said very little except that everything had gone quite well. "So, did anything special happen?" I prodded, wondering if I should just come out and ask him about the award. Finally he produced a plaque from his bag. On it was inscribed: "Communicator of the Year."

— NANCY POLLOCK

Bumper sticker: "To err is human, to forgive divine. Neither is Marine Corps policy."

— TOM FRONCEK

Fort Monmouth in New Jersey was expecting a visit from a prominent two-star general. My husband, Bob, was in charge of decorating the lawn in front of the building where the festivities were going to be held. He had arranged to have an old, retired tank and some fake land mines placed near the entrance. Bob was standing there, overseeing the task, when an uninformed passerby paused, looked over the scene and remarked to him, "Gee, I guess they're really serious about not wanting us to walk on the grass."

— KIM LABARBIERA

Another Language?

My husband was telling me about a news item he heard on National Public Radio about how the U.S. military is enlisting honeybees to find land mines. The insects are trained to react to the scent of TNT, then are fitted with transmitters and sent out to search for underground explosives. "When they smell TNT," my husband explained, "the insects hover over the area and the military tracks them to the site to safely eliminate the land mine." "Gee," I remarked, "it gives a whole new meaning to the slogan 'Be all that you can be!'"

— ANITA RAYMOND

While standing watch in the Coast Guard station in Juneau, Alaska, I got a call from the Navy in the nearby city of Adak. They had lost contact with one of their planes, and they needed the Coast Guard to send an aircraft to go find it. I asked the man where the Navy aircraft had last been spotted so we would know where to search. "I can't tell you," the Navy man said. "That's classified."

— ALFRED MILES

My youngest brother, Tony, had just completed basic training and was home on leave prior to his first tour in Germany. Since I was an Army National Guard pilot and my other brother was my crew chief, we offered to take Tony to catch his transport overseas. When we landed at McGuire Air Force Base, several of Tony's fellow privates came out to greet him. Tony ran ahead, while my other brother and I followed with his gear. As Tony approached his buddies, he was bewildered by their dumbfounded stares. Finally, he realized his friends weren't seeing his two brothers giving him a lift; they were seeing a new private arrive in his own helicopter—with his captain and sergeant carrying his bags!

— GLEN H. WILLIAMS

Stationed in Okinawa, Japan, my son and his wife were expecting their first baby. I was elated when he called me at work with the wonderful news of my grandchild's birth. I took down all the statistics and turned to relate it all to my coworkers. "I'm a grandmother!" I declared. "It's a baby girl, and she weighs five pounds." "When was she born?" someone asked. Recalling the date my son told me, I stopped, looked at the calendar and said in amazement, "Tomorrow!"

— J. M. TURK

★ ★ ★ ★ ★ ★ ★ ★ ★ ★ ★

When I was in the Coast Guard at a small boat station in Hancock, Mich., the commanding officer announced that the admiral from the 9th Coast Guard District was coming to see us the next day to speak on gender equality. Then he added, "I would like your wives to make a dish for the potluck supper."

— TODD SHAFER

A quiet evening of guard duty at Camp Pendleton, Calif., turned hairy when my son and his buddy saw a pair of luminous eyes staring back at them. It slinked toward them… a cougar. Retreating slowly, my son radioed the base. "We're being followed by a cougar," he said softly. "What do we do?" A voice responded, "Get the license plate number, and we'll send over some MPs."

— DENISE CHAFFIN

> I had just been assigned to an Air Force fighter base in Arizona. I knew the culture would be different from the Ohio logistics base where I came from. One day I was playing golf, when a ball bounced just a few feet away from me. Instead of the customary "fore!" I heard someone yell, **"Incoming!"**
>
> — ROBERT WIDO

Both my roommate and I are airborne engineer lieutenants at Fort Bragg, N.C. While we were looking for a new house to move into, we came upon a home that had a huge, open backyard. My roommate called me outside as I was inspecting the living room. "Hey, check this out," she yelled. "We've got our own drop zone back here!"

— BOB GORDON

Seen on a Coast Guard bumper sticker: "Support Search and Rescue... Get Lost!"

— CHRISTINA BURBANK

Come Again?

We were in the barracks when two guys threw down the gauntlet: 100 bucks to anyone who could do 150 push-ups. My friend disappeared into the latrine and returned minutes later, saying, "I'll take that bet." He got down on the floor and reached 50 before collapsing. "I don't get it," he said, gasping for air. "I just did 200 in the latrine."

— STEPHEN BEDICS

To bolster security at our Army post in Germany, we initiated Random Access Control Measures at our gates. This meant stopping and checking cars at various times of the day, resulting in terrible traffic. One senior officer came up with a solution: "We need more predictability in our randomness."

— JEFFREY CHURCH

Gen. George Armstrong Custer is buried on the grounds of the United States Military Academy at West Point. Since I was driving through the area, I decided to pay my respects. At the gate, the distracted young MP put down her book, checked my ID and asked the purpose of my visit. I explained that I was there to visit General Custer. As she picked up her book, she asked, "And is the general expecting you?"

— WILLIAM PARIS

Our Army unit was overseas conducting maneuvers with the Marines. On shift one night, a Marine asked my sergeant where he was from. "I'm originally from Central America," said the sergeant. "Oh, yeah?" asked the Marine. "Kansas?"

— DAVID DENBEK

The subject of the meeting was whether or not to buy a new chandelier for the sergeants' mess hall. Some officers wanted to vote on it. But one holdout opted for prudence. "Before we spend money on a chandelier," he said, "shouldn't we find out if anyone can play the thing?"

— J. STEVENS

Overheard on the Marine radio—a distress call to the Coast Guard from someone whose sailboat was taking on water: Coast Guard: "What is your position?" Distressed caller: "Vice president, State Street Bank!"

— A. KEENAN

Marine Corps pilots and aircraft maintenance technicians have a special bond. So I was unfazed when a flyboy described a vexing problem. "The radio," he said, "worked intermittently… but only sometimes."

— JAMES BULMAN

> ### File under Only in the Army.
> A sign on the telephone in our barracks read
> **"If broken, please call maintenance."**
>
> — ANDREW DRUST

★ ★ ★ ★ ★ ★ ★ ★ ★ ★ ★

While on leave, my Marine buddy and I met two nursing students from Southern California. After chatting them up awhile, the conversation turned to what we did in the service. When we told them we were in the infantry, the girls seemed very impressed, giving us big smiles as they told us how sweet that was. Since infantry and sweet are seldom used in the same sentence, I was a little confused. Until, that is, one of the girls said, "We admire any man who works with infants."

— TAEVEN THOMPSON

Imagine my surprise when I went to Tipler Army Medical Center for a heart bypass operation and discovered my surgeon's name was Dr. Eror. "What a name for a doctor," I said, not sure whether to laugh or cry. "Yeah," he agreed. "You can imagine the reaction I got when I was a major."

— GARY MEYERS

Life in the Navy is dangerous. Which is why a sign was posted on a pier at Guantanamo Bay, Cuba, reminding American sailors to "Drive Like You Work. Slow."

— DAVID HOLT

Some Reassurance

During the Cold War, I was an interpreter in the Air Force. We were testing a computer that purportedly could translate Russian into English, and vice versa. We began by uttering this English phrase, "The spirit is willing, but the flesh is weak." The Russian translation came out, "Vodka horosho, no myaca slabie." Or, in English, "The alcohol is good, but the meat is poor."

— SAM CONNOR

While in the Navy, my primary duty was to sight guns. Wanting to move up in the military, I went to law school and applied for the Judge Advocate General's Corps (JAG). My hopes of being a Navy lawyer were shot down, however, when I was rejected. It seems I suffered from poor vision.

— ALBERT MALONE

I was waiting for a flight to Texas along with four servicemen in desert camouflage uniforms. Over the top pocket of their uniform shirts was the branch of the military in which they served, followed by their last names. They were U.S. Navy, Ramirez, U.S. Army, Larkin and U.S. Army, O'Brien. The fourth man wasn't a soldier. Above his shirt pocket it read, "D.O.D. Civilian, Coward."

— WILLIAM COGGER

Our sergeant major was dimmer than a dying lightning bug. One day, I found a set of dog tags with his name on them in the shower. So, of course, I returned them. "Wow!" he said. "How'd you know they were mine?"

— JOSÉ RODRIGUEZ

Boarding a military transport plane, I noticed hydraulic fluid pouring from the tail section. "Excuse me," I said to a crew member. "Do you know the aircraft has a leak?" "Yep," he said as he continued on his way. "Aren't you concerned?" He shrugged. "Well," I asked, "how do you know when you're out of fluid?" "When it quits leaking," he answered.

— DAVID FORD

Fascinated by the military, my son went online to research everything there was to know about the armed forces, from training to equipment. Looking up bulletproof vests, he found one with an interesting warranty. It said: "Guaranteed or your money back."

— LORI SERVISS

HUH? ★ 193

Everyone knows that physical fitness and safety are paramount in the military. Which may go a long way in explaining why a recent motivational campaign produced the following poster: "Safety—Now with fewer carbs!"

— LIN ALLEN

When I was stationed at March Air Force Base (now known as March Air Reserve Base) in California, the technicians who took identification card photos were apparently fed up with complaints about the quality of the IDs. This sign was posted where it could be seen by everyone coming in for a new card: "If you want a better picture, bring a better face!"

— ED MATTSON

Hey, Medic

- ★ Stating the Obvious
- ★ Use What You Know

★ ★ ★ ★ ★ ★ ★ ★ ★ ★ ★

The time came for annual immunizations at our overseas Air Force base. To get us all vaccinated as quickly as possible, they pressed the veterinary surgeon into helping out. I got my injection from the vet. "Wow," I said, "you did that so gently, I hardly felt it." "I have to be gentle," he said. "My patients can bite."

— ANTONY MWANGI

Newly minted as an ensign, I reported for duty at the Naval medical center in San Diego, ready to follow all the rules. Expecting a no-nonsense environment, I was surprised to see a sign above the door of my new ward: "Welcome to Proctology. To expedite your visit, please back in."

— DIANE PENCE

My company was standing in line for shots and medical exams at the Naval Training Center Great Lakes. We each wore only an iodine number on our chests, and were surprised when a nurse suddenly walked in. Assessing the situation, she solved our problem when she yelled, "Close your eyes, fellows. I'm coming through."

— DANIEL RESPESS

I was new to the emergency medical branch at Fort Leonard Wood, Mo., where about ten platoon members and I were checking and stocking equipment. Suddenly a bell began to ring, and everyone dropped his equipment, grabbed his hat and headed for the exits. I did the same, scrambling to get out of the building. Concerned, I asked another soldier what was going on. "The ice-cream truck is here!" he replied.

— SUSAN HAL

★ ★ ★ ★ ★ ★ ★ ★ ★ ★ ★

After joining the Navy, my husband underwent a physical. During the exam, it was discovered that, due to a bum shoulder, he couldn't fully extend his arms above his head. Perplexed, the doctor conferred with another physician. "Let him pass," said the second doctor. "I don't see any problems unless he has to surrender."

— BETTY LEE

When I worked as a medical intern in a hospital, one of my patients was an elderly man with a thick accent. It took a while before I understood that he had no health insurance. Since he was a World War II vet, I had him transported to a VA hospital, where he'd be eligible for benefits. The next day my patient was back, along with this note from the VA admitting nurse: "Right war, wrong side."

— M. MURRAY

A hospital corpsman and I were getting an elderly retired master chief petty officer out of his wheelchair, when I noticed the man had a tattoo on his knee. "What's that?" I asked, unable to make out the design. "It's a banjo," he said sheepishly. "I'm from Alabama."

— MARY K. PARKER

As a first-time patient at a Naval dental clinic, I was looking around for the restrooms. I couldn't help but smile when I saw the sign pointing me in the right direction. It said **"Patients' heads located upstairs."**

— KEITH BROCATO

★ ★ ★ ★ ★ ★ ★ ★ ★ ★ ★

Stating the Obvious

My husband had been stationed in Europe and away from home for what seemed like years when I went for my annual gynecological checkup. My doctor asked the usual questions, including what I was using for birth control. I gave the only possible response I could: "The Atlantic Ocean."

— VICKI L. BAILEY

I was at an Air Force hospital as a second-year medical student. After assisting during a knee surgery, the nurse anesthetist and I were having trouble waking the patient. Our staff physician, however, knew what to do. "Marine," he shouted, "this is Colonel Smith." The patient then promptly sat straight up on the gurney and replied, "Sir!"

— 2ND LT. JOSHUA CAREY

My father-in-law, a retired Army officer, was recently in the hospital for surgery, and on the day of his operation, I went to wish him luck. I quickly found out he hadn't lost his military bearing—or his sense of humor. After I knocked, I heard him call out, "Friend or enema?"

— DEBORAH MARTIN

As a members of an Air Force Reserve medical unit, we worked with nurses just out of nursing school who were not used to military ranks. This notice appeared on our bulletin board: "There will be a meeting of all junior officers at 1300 hours today. If you are not sure if you are a junior officer, plan on attending."

— MARY SCHMIDT

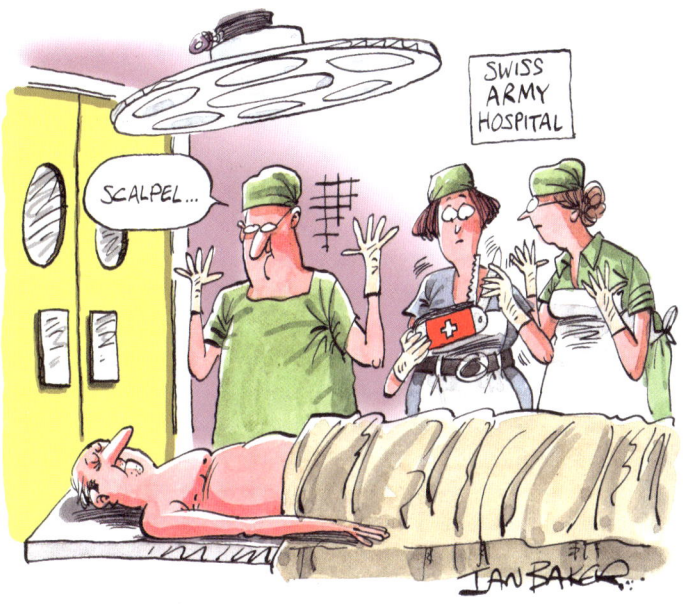

During the time I was a first lieutenant at Seymour Johnson Air Force Base in North Carolina, the junior officers challenged the senior officers to see who would donate the most blood. After trying several times to locate a vein in my left arm, the technician applied a Band-Aid, then inserted a needle into my right arm, and after drawing blood, put a bandage on that arm as well. As I left the collection facility, I passed a colonel. Noting my two bandages, he looked at me and shook his head, saying, "I knew you young guys would find a way to cheat."

— JAMES H. DILDA

★ ★ ★ ★ ★ ★ ★ ★ ★ ★ ★

There was a long-standing practice at our hospital in Virginia that physicians with a rank of major or above did not have to rotate through nighttime emergency-room duty. A new commanding officer, however, issued an order that all physicians, regardless of rank, must take ER call. On his first night of emergency-room duty, our pathologist, a major, had to see a colonel's wife who was complaining of abdominal pain. "I'll try to evaluate you as best as I can," he said after introducing himself. "But I must inform you that you are the first living patient I've seen in fifteen years."

— JAMES R. RAYMOND, M.D.

When I entered the Army medical center on base 20 minutes prior to delivering my baby, I had a hard time convincing the staff that I was definitely in the last stages of labor. We had waited 10 minutes in the pre-admittance area when a nurse finally came in and said, "My name is Captain Smith, but you can call me Lisa." "I'm Chaplain Barclay," my husband responded, "but you can call me Kleet." "My name is Holly," I added in frustration, "but in a few minutes you can call me Mom!"

— HOLLY BARCLAY

While working as a Navy nurse in a military hospital's emergency room, I was required to introduce myself by my rank and full name. I usually refer to myself as Ensign Mike Payne, but one busy day I rushed into a patient's room and blurted, "Hi, I'm Ensign Payne." "Hi," the patient responded. "I'm in some pain, too."

— MIKE PAYNE

★ ★ ★ ★ ★ ★ ★ ★ ★ ★ ★

Use What You Know

While assigned to the Naval Medical Center in San Diego, I overheard this conversation between a pharmacy technician and a sergeant who needed a prescription filled for his son. Technician: "How old is your boy?" Sergeant: "Three months." Technician: "What's his weight?" Sergeant: "About two M-16s." Technician: "Loaded or unloaded?"

— MARCELO BUNDANG

As a physical therapist, I was working with a retired Army colonel. During part of his rehab, I had him walk back and forth while facing me the entire time. "Colonel," I joked, "you walk better backward than forward." "Yeah," he deadpanned. "My battalion retreated a lot."

— JENNIFER SEKULA

The scale at our clinic in Iraq was pitiful. Just to get it working properly required plenty of kicking and stomping. One day, as I was going through my weighing-in routine, a medic walked by. Watching as I pounded the scale with my feet, he wondered aloud, "Killing the messenger?"

— DAWN NEHLS

An odd thing happened when I contacted the Navy about my health care: They said their records listed me as "deceased." The petty officer I spoke to was very helpful and input my current information into the computer. But a window popped up and balked: "Are you sure you want to resurrect Joseph S. Clein?"

— JOSEPH S. CLEIN

★ ★ ★ ★ ★ ★ ★ ★ ★ ★ ★

As an Army dentist, one day I treated a general on base. During his visit I had to make impressions of his teeth, and the puttylike substance I used smeared all over his lips and cheeks. After I was done I invited him over to the sink, gave him a moist towel and asked him to "clean up the mess I made" while I filled out the lab report. When I turned back around, my heart skipped a beat as I watched the general wipe up the counter around the sink.

— LT. COL. WILLIAM C. ELTON

During a visit to a military medical clinic, I was sent to the lab to have blood drawn. The technician there was friendly and mentioned that his mood improved every day because he was due to leave the service in two months. As he placed the tourniquet on my arm, he told me that taking the blood wouldn't hurt much. Then, noticing my Air Force T-shirt, he asked me what my husband did. When I replied that he was a recruiter, the technician smiled slyly and said, "This might hurt a little more than I thought."

— SHERRI VINIARD

> While visiting a VA hospital with my son, I overheard a retired Army sergeant asking people which branch of the military they'd served in. Some said Army, a few Navy, others Air Force. "What were you in?" she asked a man who'd just entered the room. Confused, he mumbled, **"The bathroom."**
>
> — SUSAN LOPSHIRE

★ ★ ★ ★ ★ ★ ★ ★ ★ ★ ★

Going through some of my grandfather's old books, I found a *Serviceman's Spiritual Handbook* from World War II. "I didn't know Pop Pop was in World War II," I said to my father. "Where was he stationed?" "He was in the Army at Cape Hatteras, assigned as a lookout to watch for German U-boats," my father replied. "So he was never in active combat abroad?" I queried. "That's right," my father answered. "The Army didn't think his eyesight was good enough."

— SARAH B. PAUL

Two weeks after having a vasectomy, I was discussing the procedure with a friend who was going to have one, too. "It was quick outpatient surgery," I assured him, "although I did experience some minor complications because of infection." He looked worried, so I tried to lighten the mood. "Hey, I only paid $15 for the operation after insurance—I guess you get what you pay for." "Oh, no," he exclaimed in alarm. "I'm having mine done at the Naval hospital—and it's free!"

— STEVE M. WHALEN

The military is a stickler for rules, and when it comes to off-base medical treatment, the rules are that many procedures need to be preauthorized. So when we were expecting our first child, my husband and I did things by the book. After our son was born on September 22, the insurance statement showed that the obstetrician was not paid the full contracted amount. So I called our insurer's representative. "The problem is, your son was born early," she said, looking through my files. "And the Air Force hadn't authorized him to arrive for another two weeks."

— AMY AMSDEN

★ ★ ★ ★ ★ ★ ★ ★ ★ ★ ★ ★

I didn't enlist in the Army—I was drafted. So I wasn't going to make life easy for anyone. During my physical, the doctor asked softly, "Can you read the letters on the wall?" "What letters?" I answered slyly. "Good," said the doctor. "You passed the hearing test."

— ROBERT DUPREY

RANK
and FiLE

★ **Pulling Rank**

★ **A Rose Is a Rose**

★ ★ ★ ★ ★ ★ ★ ★ ★ ★ ★

Reporting to Camp Lejeune, I was glad my husband had already explained to me that a "Commissioned Officers Mess (open)" is open to all officers, whereas a "Commissioned Officers Mess (closed)" is limited to officers residing on base. Therefore, I understood this message: "During the holidays the Commissioned Officers Mess (open) will be closed. The Commissioned Officers Mess (closed) will be open."

— PATRICIA W. MINER

My cousin, a senior airman in the Air Force, and my brother-in-law, a Marine sergeant, were comparing their experiences in the Saudi Arabian desert. They commiserated about the heat, sand and food. But when my Air Force cousin grumbled about the uncomfortable beds and the small tents, my Marine brother-in-law looked surprised. His astonishment grew as my cousin went on to complain about the unreliable air-conditioning and meager choice of cable channels. Finally the Marine spoke up: "Tents? You had tents!"

— A. K. MCNEILL

The theater group at our Navy base delayed the opening curtain until well after the 8 P.M. starting time because the commanding officer was still conspicuously absent from his reserved front-row seat. Since we were all aware of military protocol, everyone waited patiently. When a member of our drama club finally spotted the captain settling into his seat, we quickly dimmed the lights. That's when we heard the captain proclaim to his wife, "Great luck! We made it just in time."

— LEE R. FEATHERINGHAM

While visiting our daughter Susan, who was stationed at Fort Hood Army Base, we joined her at the officers club. Upon entering the building, Susan hung her cap in the hall, and I asked her if she wasn't afraid that someone might take it. "No, I'm not worried," she said, sighing. "No one wants to be a second lieutenant."

— DOROTHY THOMPSON

After being at sea in the Persian Gulf for 90 straight days, I went to the squadron command master chief to complain. "Chief, I joined the Navy to see the world," I said, "but for the past three months all I've seen is water." "Lieutenant," he replied, "three-quarters of the earth is covered with water, and the Navy has been showing you that. If you wanted to see the other quarter, you should have joined the Army."

— PAUL NEWMAN

I was scolding our pastor for his habit of starting church services five or ten minutes late. I mentioned that in my years with the Air Force, when the general scheduled us to take off at 0700 hours, he didn't mean 0705 or 0710. The pastor smiled at me and said, "My general outranks your general."

— BOB BALTZELL

While visiting my son on his Army base, I chatted with a colleague of his. "What rank are you?" I asked. "I'm relieved to say that I've just been promoted from captain to major." "Relieved? Why?" "Because," he replied, **"my last name is Hook."**

— BARBARA BLACKBURN

When we agreed to help our sergeant move to a new apartment, we didn't know the elevator wasn't working. So after hours of carrying heavy boxes and furniture up 11 floors, we were wiped out. And when the sergeant asked us to search for his favorite pot, no one moved. "I'll give a bottle of Scotch to whoever finds it," he shouted. Within minutes, a private found the pot. "Good," said the sarge. "Now look for the Scotch."

— WOO-KI SOHNN

Todd, my son, joined the Marines. When he went to take the placement and physical exams, he was in a room full of candidates for all the military services. Todd overheard someone near him say, "Aren't the Marines just a department of the Navy?" "Yes," came the response. "They're the men's department."

— EMILY MURPHY

When my husband was reassigned to Fort Knox, in Kentucky, he was told we couldn't live together off base. Instead, he'd have to stay in the barracks with the other grunts. My husband begged his sergeant to clear up the matter. But it was no use. "Son," said his sergeant, "if the Army wanted you to have a wife, we would have issued you one."

— DIANE RAY

★ ★ ★ ★ ★ ★ ★ ★ ★ ★ ★

Pulling Rank

The enlisted guys may have won the annual softball game against the officers, but they lost the public relations war. Here's how I wrote it up for our naval base's Plan of the Day: "The officers powered their way to a second-place finish, while the noncoms managed to finish next to last."

— DAVID FRIEL

During a staff meeting at the Air Force base, the captain disagreed with everything being discussed. The commander, a general, grew annoyed, and let the younger officer know it. "Well, sir," said the captain, "I doubt you made general by agreeing with everything someone else recommended." "That's true," said the general, leaning in. "But that is how I made major."

— HAROLD R. LONGMIRE

My husband works in the fuels squadron at an Air Force base, and many of his coworkers complain about the superior attitude of the pilots. One day the fuel guys decided to put things in perspective for the proud pilots. They all came to work wearing shirts inscribed, "Without fuel, pilots are pedestrians."

— AMBER ANDERSON

Officer candidate school at Fort Sill, Oklahoma, was tough. During an inspection, a fellow soldier received 30 demerits for a single penny found within his area. Ten demerits were for "valuables insecure," ten because the penny wasn't shined, and ten because Abraham Lincoln needed a shave.

— JACK HOWELL

My brother Ken was home on leave from his post in Hawaii, when he announced that he had just been promoted to lieutenant commander. We were all pleased with the news, but some of us less knowledgeable about military rankings asked Ken to explain what the promotion meant. After several failed attempts to get us to understand, he sighed and said, "Before, I was Hawkeye Pierce, and now I'm Frank Burns." Expressions of understanding immediately lit the room.

— JACQUELYN MILLER

Our patient in the hospital was a big, burly former officer. Just after surgery, and still half out of it, he became agitated and confused, tearing at his IVs and trying to escape his bed. The nurses gamely attempted to keep him calm, but were losing this battle. That's when my old Air Force training came in handy. "Colonel!" I commanded. "At ease." And with that, the colonel fell back to sleep.

— PATTY ANDREWS

My daughter, Emily, was telling a friend that her brother, Chris, was training to become a Navy submariner. The friend, who had just been assigned to a Navy destroyer, good-naturedly called Chris a Bubblehead. Later I related the story to Chris and asked if he'd heard the term. He said he had and added, "We also have a name for people who work on destroyers." "What is it?" I asked. "Targets."

— JO BARKER

 **I've got attention deficit disorder, Sarge.**

As a young Navy recruit, I discovered early on where I stood in the chain of command after stepping on a cockroach. "What have you just done?" demanded a petty officer who was walking by. "Just killed a cockroach, sir," I answered. "Next time salute it first. They have more time in the Navy than you do."

— TOM MAY

★ ★ ★ ★ ★ ★ ★ ★ ★ ★

A Rose Is a Rose

As a benefits specialist in the Marines, I traveled around delivering lectures on life insurance. After listening to a dozen of these talks, the corporal who drove me from base to base insisted he knew my entire spiel by heart. "Prove it," I said. So at the next base the corporal delivered the speech. As he ended his flawless performance, a Marine asked, "What do I pay for insurance after I leave the Corps?" My driver froze. Was the jig up? Would ignorance of the facts force him to crumble? Not my corporal! "Marine," he said sternly, as he pointed to me, "that is such a dumb question that I am going to let my driver answer it."

— E. M. CROSSMAN

As a fluid-dynamics engineer, I was invited to give a lecture at a classified meeting attended by military officials. To break the ice, I began my talk with a joke. Several days later, at a restaurant, I ran into a naval officer who had heard my speech. "Would you mind repeating that joke here?" he asked. "That way it won't be considered confidential anymore, and I can tell it to others."

— PHILIP DIWAKAR

When I was stationed at Tinker Air Force Base in Oklahoma, we had a sergeant who made sure everyone knew who was boss. "You have one stripe on your arm, and I have four," he yelled in the face of one airman third class. "That makes you nothing! So when I bark, I expect you to move. Because I'm in charge!" "Big deal," said the unimpressed airman. "A sergeant in charge of nothing."

— MARVIN WARD

Sixty years ago, the Japanese surrendered, bringing World War II to an end. One of the heroes of the war was Chester Nimitz. At a postwar speech, the admiral recounted this story: "As an ensign, I told a sailor to put himself on report for wearing an extremely dirty uniform. I watched the daily report list, but the sailor's name never appeared. When I ran into the man again, I yelled, 'Didn't I order you to put yourself on report?' 'Aye, aye, sir,' said the sailor. 'But after mulling it over, I decided to give myself another chance.'"

— ALBERT VITO

Officiating at an Air Force wedding, I was impressed with how meticulous the groom and his attendants looked in their formal uniforms. The bride's brother, a Coast Guard officer candidate, arrived just before the start of the ceremony. There was a gasp as he took his place beside the others, donning a pair of white gloves, which were standard for his uniform. The gloveless Air Force officers were embarrassed by this inconsistency among the men. "Not to worry," assured the proud but outnumbered brother, as he removed his gloves. "My senior officer told me if this happened, I should lower my sights to comply with Air Force standards."

— REV. PAUL W. ATWATER

An annual survey among my fellow junior officers indicated that lack of communication from our superiors was a big problem. The commanding officer, however, refused to believe the results. "If communication is really so bad," he demanded of his department heads, "why am I only hearing about it now?"

— RICKEY RUFFIN

Military cost-cutting has hit everything, including toilet paper. Only the cheapest graces our latrines. So when a couple of boxes filled with the good stuff—two-ply tissue!—fell in our laps, it was like manna from heaven. But the next morning, our behinds were brought down to Earth. It was all a mistake. The boxes had been intended for the officers club. "I should have known," grumbled the supply sergeant. "Our officers demand everything in duplicate!"

— GARY WINTER

No one on my uncle's troop ship was particularly upset when a much-loathed sergeant went overboard. No one except the captain. "How did this happen?" he demanded, as the sergeant dried off. "That's the wrong question, sir," yelled a sailor. "Try asking him whether he was pushed or shoved.

— MALCOLM ELVY

My brother-in-law, Steve, and one of his fellow soldiers were assigned to wax the floors of their barracks. They'd heard that if they got the wax really hot, it would just glide across the floor, cutting their labor time in half. Unfortunately, as they were heating the can of wax with a cigarette lighter, it caught on fire, setting off alarms and attracting fire trucks, ambulances and the police. Steve had to report to his sergeant's office immediately. Assuming he was in big trouble, he took a deep breath as he faced his superior. But before Steve could say a word, the sergeant simply muttered, "Been there, done that. You're free to go."

— JEREMY NOBLE

Art Credits

Ian Baker *134, 199*
David Brown *37, 113*
Patrick Byrnes *121*
John Caldwell *27*
Dave Carpenter *20, 92, 104, 127, 191*
Ken Catalino *5, 211*

Joe DiChiarro *146*
Ralph Hagen *101, 156*
Dan Reynolds *49, 87, 163*
Steve Smeltzer *15, 53, 76, 177*
Thomas Bros. *44, 66*
Kim Warp *63, 186*

Cover Art: *George McKeon*

★ ★ ★ ★ ★ ★ ★ ★ ★ ★ ★ ★

If you have enjoyed this book or it has touched your life in some way, we would love to hear from you.

Please send your comments to:
Hallmark Book Feedback
P.O. Box 419034
Mail Drop 215
Kansas City, MO 64141

Or e-mail us at:
booknotes@hallmark.com

★ ★ ★ ★ ★ ★ ★ ★ ★ ★ ★ ★